The Journey into the *Myst*

A true story of the paranormal

(Volume I of the *Myst* series)

by Drs. Alex and David Bennet

Volume I: Journey into the *Myst*
Volume II: Patterns in the *Myst*
Volume III: The Mind and the *Myst*

MQIPress (2020)
Frost, West Virginia
ISBN 978-1-949829-29-7

The human experience is a neuronal dance with the Universe.

Original version of Parts I and II (as eBooks) 2013
First Printing soft cover 2020
Copyright © 2020 MQIPress. All rights reserved.

MQIPress
Frost, West Virginia
303 Mountain Quest Lane
Marlinton, WV 24954
United States of America
Telephone: 304-799-7267

alex@mountainquestinstitute.com
www.mountainquestinstitute.com
www.mountainquestinn.com
www.MQIPress.com
www.Myst-art.com

ISBN 978-1-949829-29-7

Nestled between Earth and Sky, Day and Night,

Lies a mystical realm where past and present meet the future.

For each of us there is a Gate to open, a Threshold to cross,

Where timeless truths remind us, we are not alone.

Volume 1

Table of Contents

Preface

David:

In this book we try to **brighten the unfamiliar path and encourage everyone to explore and realize that we all travel the path of oneness**, that is, the recognition that we are all interconnected and part of the same life force opening to the fullness of who we are. No matter how many detours we make we're all heading in the same direction … we just have different ways of exploring, learning, being and growing.

We live on this wonderful farm in a high valley of the West Virginia Allegheny Mountains that is home to the Mountain Quest Institute (MQI) as well as the Mountain Quest Inn and Retreat Center. See www.mountainquestinn.com and www.mountainquestinstitute.com At MQI our research is focused on the Triangle of Life, that is, science, humanism and spirituality, and we find no conflict among these three. Perhaps that statement is even truer since the miracle occurred and the Myst arrived.

But we're going to share this true story with you, though it might be good to give you a preview so you have an idea where the story is going. In the Fall of 2011 Mountain Quest hosted the Fall Festival (Frost Fest), complete with a corn maze and tents full of games, food and crafts. We set up a booth of *Myst*-Art, highlighting a framed 8"x10" pictured we called "Evening Prayers." The person who gave the best explanation of what was in the picture would win it!

(Above) "Evening Prayers," the Myst photograph that was highlighted at the 2011 Frost Fest event hosted by Mountain Quest Institute.

Dozens of people ranging from aged 10 to 80 stopped to look at the picture and take a few minutes to describe what they saw. Below are some of those descriptions. We start with those with a philosophical bent:

"The Proof! Almost heaven, West Virginia"

"Mother Earth's evening breath"

"Life: Straight line for some; foggy for all; ending in a beautiful sunset."

These were our three top winners, who each received an 8"x10" photograph. But all of the descriptions were good, so we wound up giving each of these entrants a 5"x7" photograph. Here are a few descriptions that are more **narrative in nature**:

> "I see a lady who may have been the owner of this land at one time. To me, she is watching over the wild life such as a bear that once roamed the land. She will always be here and will always be mother and keeper of the land. An angel is always with her."

> "I see a beaver-like creature coming out of the ground warning the beings/fairies of the day that the sun is leaving. I can see that from his coming they slowly pull away, disappearing with the sun."

> "Spirit animals coming home at sunset."

> "I think it looks like a spirit celebration. Bottom one on right looks like a conductor, with hands up like he is conducting an orchestra; and the ones playing music are higher. We all are spiritual in nature to some degree. When we feel joy and love, we often connect our spiritual beliefs with that joy and love."

> "Trumpets, angel wings, a woman praying, three angels, one with outstretched arms."

Another theme of descriptions was related to the Indian tribes who used to roam this land, which is on a Cherokee Hunting Trail. Observers aware of the trail described:

> "A warrior's stallion just coming back from a victory battle. He's bowing down to his rider with triumph!"

> "A male warrior, an Indian with his animal spirit. Profile of face with a feather in the hair wearing a leather/fur shawl with his animal spirit, the cougar. The cougar with mouth open lunges into the sky with his warrior."

By the way, the description included in the *Myst*-Art galleries alludes to the spiritual nature of the Earth. It reads: **"As the sun goes down elemental earth energies connect with celestial possibilities over the fence to eternity."**

So, these are some descriptions of what others think of the picture. And what do I think, as a man who spent his life as an electronics technician, a nuclear physicist, a neuroscientist, and as a CEO and Chairman of the Board of an engineering consulting firm and Co-Founder of the Mountain Quest Institute? Ah, but let the story unfold.

The Drs. Alex and David Bennet live at the Mountain Quest Institute, Inn and Retreat Center situated on a 430-acre farm in the Allegheny Mountains of West Virginia. See www.mountainquestinn.com and www.mountainquestinstitute.com For information call 304-799-7267. Alex may be contacted at alex@mountainquestinstitute.com

Chapter 1: The Miracle

Alex:

What we are about to tell you would have been quite unbelievable to me before this journey began. It is not a story of the reality either of us has known for well over our 60 and 70 years of age, but rather, the reality of dreams and fairytales.

From my viewpoint, my life's journey has moved through a myriad of bumps and breaks, always somehow mending itself and moving through new and interesting turns and twists. I've had the opportunity to sing on the outdoor stage of the Metropolitan Opera, live and work abroad, serve as the Chief Knowledge Officer of the U.S. Department of the Navy, and research and publish books with my partner. We've written a myriad of material focused around knowledge, learning and change. Oh, yes, I've been on the internal journey—an exploration of the inner self, the unconscious—for many years as well. But that journey has always been tucked safely away from the outside world. Although no doubt the inner journey has significantly influenced my thoughts and feelings, it has not visibly danced around the events of my external world! Until now!

This story we write is perhaps even more difficult for my partner to put into words. David is by education a nuclear physicist and mathematician, teaching many years ago at the U.S. Navy Nuclear Power School under the legendary Admiral Rickover. David is an incessant learner, collecting knowledges along the way, with many degrees and credentials punctuating an active business life.

Alex and David Bennet at their high valley farm in the Allegheny Mountains of West Virginia.

Our journey into the *Myst* came with the Summer of 2010. In these latter years, like many in our generation, we are becoming more sensitive to our physical health. So after various friends and colleagues mentioned the value of a colonoscopy as a preventive measure for cancer, David decided to have one. The procedure proceeded on a Friday without any surprises. He was in; he was out … quick and relatively painless, sort of a "check the list" kind of thing in terms of preventative medicine.

It was quite a surprise when he woke me the following Tuesday early in the morning, quite a matter-of-factly reporting that he was bleeding heavily. The hospital of choice is 62 miles away from our country inn and farm; that's about one hour and thirty minutes through winding two-lane country roads. We decided not to wait for the doctor's office to open but to leave immediately heading towards the emergency room. To pull up the memory is as if it is happening again, now.

In the driver's seat as the sun is rising, I weave my way through the turns and curves, around trees and cow pastures occasionally punctuated by a farmhouse. We make it about half way to the hospital. In the front passenger seat, David is experiencing considerable pressure and pain, and says he cannot hold it; he feels like he is exploding and insists I pull the car over to the side of the road. It is early in the morning, with no houses nearby; no cars; no people. I pull over. David gets out of the car and goes about 10 feet into tall grass. As a liter of blood and light tissue explode out of him, he passes out and falls to the ground.

Watching from the car, I quickly jump out and run to him, shaking him, yelling at him to wake up. David is white and clammy, going into shock. I grab his arm and start pulling him up, then reach under his shoulders and drag him toward the car. He becomes conscious for about 10 seconds as I attempt to get him in the front seat of the car. He helps. As I run around the front of the car to the driver's seat, David pulls up on the lever to the right of the seat, releasing his seat backwards and down. His head is leaning back against the head rest as fluids start gurgling up in his throat. I am afraid he will drown in his own juices. I yell, "No!", and reach across to pull the seat back up. As his head rises it begins to fall to the side.

I talk to David as I release the car break to move forward, "Stay with me." But he is not able to stay conscious. His head lolls to the right; and blood is dripping onto the seat of the car. It is too much, too much blood. I see the moisture on his white face vividly. He is in shock. The hospital is 30 miles away.

I know we are at a critical life point, a juncture, a time of choice. It is that moment that all of us know is coming yet seems to arrive unexpectedly. As I press my foot to the gas, **I scream to my guides and guardian angels with every cell in my body, I demand, "I need help! I need help now!"** This cry is the last thing David hears before losing consciousness.

I focus on the road ahead, speeding the car up and swinging around an S curve. My only thoughts are to move, to drive toward help. As I come out of the S curve, there, by the right side of the road in front of us, less than a mile from where David first fell, sits an ambulance, a rescue squad vehicle, and a fire engine. As I pull over, I see a tow truck to the left, with three or four men standing in a circle chatting, watching the tow truck pull an abandoned car out of a ditch.

The tableau is surreal; I cannot fathom it. Now on automatic response, I throw the driver's door open, hop out, wave my hands, and scream for help. Three men race across the road and pull David out of the car onto a magically appearing gurney. Within minutes David is stabilized, and awake.

The ambulance driver leans toward me as the attendant inside the ambulance prepares David for transport. "I didn't know why we were here," he shares softly. "But now I know." He then asks, "Can you follow the ambulance?" "Yes" I respond, and the race to the hospital continues.

David:

Have you ever been a patient in an intensive care unit (ICU)? I have. Once for a fibrillating heart that was fixed by an easy operation, and the second from the loss of blood that Alex just described. I was lucky—or helped by outside forces—or both. Lying in a hospital bed where you can do nothing but what you are told leads you to either rebel or succumb to patience. Without realizing it, I was trained by daily commuting in the Washington, D.C. area that given two choices—(1) to rebel and try to change the world and fail, or (2) to not to worry about what you cannot change—the latter choice is almost always the best. Simply redirect your thoughts to something more productive.

Back to the ICU. I was weak, relaxed and conscious, with nothing to do but think about things that seemed important. Clearly this experience had been a close call, but was it luck, fate or synchronicity that chose to put me in the ICU instead of underground and perhaps in the spiritual world? This was not the first time that I had a close call with a life/death outcome. As I reflect, I can remember a number of situations where if things had been a little bit different I would not be writing this story. Luck, chance, destiny, help from above—I just don't know.

For the past decade Alex and I have defined and studied, given workshops and lectures, written books and published papers, on knowledge and its sources, meaning and application. Our focus has been on the ability to take effective action, that is, given current situation "A" and a desired situation "B", having the knowledge such that the decisions you make and actions you take change situation "A" into situation "B". Since we can only influence the world by our actions, our definition of knowledge becomes critical to surviving in a changing, uncertain and complex world.[1]

One thing we have learned is that "absolute" knowledge is not something we humans are likely to possess. We simply do not live long enough in time nor travel far enough in space to validate any knowledge as "absolute." This is a very important conclusion to me, because it means that it is *wiser* to keep an *open* and *inquisitive* mind when we run across events and phenomena that appear to conflict with, or contradict, our past experiences and/or current beliefs.

When I was 12 years old I read a book called *The Rise of the New Physics* by Albert Einstein and Leopold Enfield. I understood only a small part of it, but was fascinated by everything I read. I decided then and there that I wanted to be a physicist when I grew up so that I could understand how the world worked (so I thought). It was more than 24 years before I graduated with a Bachelors in Math and a Bachelors and Masters in Physics from the University of Texas.

What I have learned about physics is that as beautiful, valuable, and insightful as it is—from Newtonian Mechanics to Quantum Mechanics and Einstein's two ingenious relativity theories—*there are many things in our Universe that are still incomprehensible*. Our limitations of understanding become clear when we ask questions about foundational concepts such as time, space, energy or even the meaning of our theories, experiments or actions.

All too often we form beliefs—from learning and from our experience, goals and fears, etc.—that tend to solidify in our brains and become absolutes that are "who we are" and, often subconsciously, we must defend at all costs. Where it applies, the scientific method is excellent for those phenomena. But yes, science has boundaries of its knowledge and applications. It also has limits to its understanding and methodology. It also has contradictions within its findings, and has to live, at least temporarily, with some incomprehensible results.

The challenge arises, however, when we discover aspects of our Universe that do not succumb to the methods of scientific validation, things that lie beyond the boundaries of current scientific understanding and capabilities for validation. An example is the phenomenon of meditation. How does one validate that the process and results of meditation are what the meditator says they are? One can never exactly "repeat" the results, and there can be no objectivity to the outcome. The scientific method is simply not applicable … yet. However, as the Dali Lama has offered: "If 10,000 monks can meditate over 3,000 years and all of them say that they get similar results, one should give these results some credibility." As distinct from scientific truth, the Dali Lama calls this *rational inference*.

All of these thoughts were on my mind while I was in the ICU. And my thoughts just kept rambling. So many of us tend to take a stand that says "I am right—you are wrong" or "I know and you do not know." I have found very few things that support these dichotomies. Things are never—or rarely—either right or wrong, yes or no, good or bad, black or white, true or false. The Universe isn't so simple. As we delved down into understanding knowledge, we discovered that knowledge is context sensitive and situation dependent. Simplification can be very valuable—or it can be disastrous.

Why did all of these thoughts keep moving through my mind? It clearly had something to do with the remarkable events that brought me to the ICU.

Of the unusual occurrences in my life, until recently the main one was a precognition of an automobile accident that actually occurred 10 minutes later. As a motorcyclist came off of a short pier in Newport Rhode Island, the motorcycle fell over and the driver's body was thrown into the brick wall of a restaurant 10 feet in front of my car. While the outcome is in the police records, my sensing the accident remains a personal experience and cannot be verified externally. But "I" vividly remember that ten minutes before the accident when I touched the door handle of the car sitting in a parking lot four miles from the scene of the accident, my gut said "there is going to be an automobile accident." This could sound crazy if we knew what time was. But, in fact, even today we do not understand what time, space, energy or even a vacuum are.

In a sense we as humans have done ourselves a huge disfavor by separating our world into areas of knowledge such as science, philosophy, religion and spirituality. While specialization certainly guides research, it also labels people and tends to limit our thinking, thereby sometimes creating walls or stovepipes that result in languages, beliefs and ownerships that make interactions, combinations and synergistic thinking difficult if not impossible. Am I repeating myself? Am I getting ahead of the story?

As I lay on the hospital bed getting blood transfusions and wondering how long I would need to be here, I thought about the road not taken. I would like to stay here on planet Earth and continue to achieve what Alex and I consider our purpose for being, that is, learning, understanding and contributing where we can to the forward march and quality of human development. I could perhaps live another 20 years, and share with others our lessons learned, our thoughts, ideas and experiences. Or perhaps I could slide quietly into the night, my atoms continuing on their 13 billion year life history by separating and once again going out into space and wondering around until the Universe comes to its end.

Or perhaps there is a third road, a non-physical part of our world that is compatible with us yet exists under different "rules and laws" than our material world has provided. Do souls live forever? Are angels real? Are psychics really psychic? I do not know the answers to these questions, but I do know that sometimes this world demonstrates amazing things that appear impossible from a purely material viewpoint.

Perhaps the appearance of the ambulance was luck, perhaps it was a Cosmic determination, who knows? In any case, after three days of deep reflection I was able to leave the ICU. But I left with the dramatic memories of my close call floating in my awareness, and a deeper feeling of how little I knew about our world. Do you realize how many things and happenings lay right in front of us yet we have so much trouble seeing, feeling, sensing and comprehending them? The easy path invites our direction. The safest stand makes us feel good. Any new direction on "the path not taken" scares us. Perhaps the light of the unknown is so low that many of us choose the better-known, common path that we can easily see, understand and follow. Or do we dare to grow, run risks, question the unquestionable and keep an open but cautious and learning mind.

Clearly the Universe recognized that both Alex and I needed time to reflect on these events. I had fallen in a Poison Oak patch, and Alex had pulled me out of the patch. As if that wasn't enough, I caught a Staph infection during those three days in ICU and Alex, who was with me sleeping in a chair beside my bed, had a spot on her left forearm. The next few weeks we were forced to slow down and focus on healing our bodies.

Chapter 2: The Road to Recovery

Happy, Alex sat in the white rocker on the porch of the old farm house, slowly moving back and forth, eyes focused on the large field to the left. The horses had sensed something in the next field; their heads were turned that direction as they stood silently at attention. Then there was a snort signaling, a release of sorts, and they all went about the business of living. Visuelle, the beautiful black Polish Arabian who was the mother of three of the youngsters, went down for a roll in a dusty spot despite her advancing age. Her three offspring—Mountain Quest (Mounty), Harmony Quest and Mystical Quest—grazed nearby. Vision, a stunning brown and white Quarter Horse, glided at a slow trot over to the water trough. The others were out of sight.

(Above) From left to right, Harmony, Mystical, Vision and Mounty,
all part of the Mountain Quest family.

Despite the warmth of the July day, Alex was covered from head to foot, a tribute to the Poison Oak that covered much of her body and a blotch of Staph infection on the inside of her left forearm. But "life is good, life is good, life is good" bounced rhythmically through her head in time to the rocking.

David cracked the front door, "It's about time for our second set of showers. I just put the sheets and morning clothes in the dryer."

Alex pushed up out of the chair, catching his eyes as she moved toward him, then breaking out into a smile. David gave a soft pat to her rear as she preceded him up the stairs. They were alive. David was regaining his health. Life was good, life was good.

David:

I had been told by my doctor that a full recovery would take at least six months, probably nine. But, of course, I believed I could recover within three months. I was wrong. While I felt much better after leaving the ICU, I didn't like all the time it took to care for the staph infection and the poison oak. Okay, it was necessary, but I didn't have to like it, just do it.

So, it took a while for things to settle down to normal—if there is such a thing as normality at our 430-acre farm, 12-room inn, conference center and research institute. There are always many things needing to be done, ranging from caring for the 12 horses, 3 Llamas, goats and 6 Longhorn cattle, to welcoming and exchanging ideas with guests, doing dishes, facilitating an executive retreat, preparing for a wedding, or finishing a research article for publication. Fortunately, we both have learned that physical exercise, good nutrition, using the mind actively in different ways, and having something you "believe is worth doing to make the world a better place" are the ground rules for a long and healthy life.

Having been given a go-ahead (through luck or miracle), I was impatient to get back to "normal." But I couldn't put aside the vivid reminder of the fragility of life and the importance of learning and making life worthwhile for as many others as possible through learning, sharing thinking, writing and actions. There is only one past for each of us, yet the future is normally thought of as unknowable, but perhaps fathomable. During this recovery period from the ER experience, Alex and I both felt thankful, relieved and thoughtful about our own lives as well as life from a planetary perspective.

How unique each of us is … and how wonderful to have the opportunity to live and experience so many facets of humanity. We frequently talked about science, spirituality and humanism, and began to realize that these were not parts of three different realities; rather, three views or perspectives of one Reality. But that area of research would have to wait for another time in our lives. Two new surprises were on the horizon, soon to impact our lives and expand and challenge our perspectives.

Alex:

At the end of July, I was scheduled to attend a week-long program at The Monroe Institute (TMI) situated in Faber, Virginia, along the Shenandoah Mountains. Actually, the program was *Starlines I*, an incredible exploration through the inner landscape of the mystery and majesty of energy systems throughout the Milky Way galaxy (and beyond).

For that to make sense, maybe I should talk a bit about TMI.[2] It is certainly an unusual place. This is the home of Hemi-Sync®, that's a registered trademark short name for hemispheric synchronization, the use of sound coupled with a binaural beat to bring both hemispheres of the brain into unison (Bennet and Bennet, 2007).[3] What can happen during hemispheric synchronization is a physiologically reduced state of arousal while maintaining conscious awareness, and the capacity to reach the unconscious creative state through the window of consciousness. In short, this is having your conscious mind awake/aware while you are exploring your unconscious landscape. Sound like fun? It's amazing; and for many people it really works! I'm one of those many people.

I learned about TMI while I was still working with the Department of Navy, developing models for what we called "Knowing: The Art of War 2000." We recognized that as we moved away from predictable warfare patterns susceptible to logic, our leaders were increasingly reliant on their "gut" instinct, an internal sense of "knowing." Our concept of knowing focused on the cognitive capabilities of observing and perceiving a situation, the cognitive processing that must occur to understand the external world and make maximum use of our internal thinking capabilities, and the mechanism for creating deep knowledge and acting on that knowledge, using the Self as an Agent of Change.[4]

A bright Ph.D. from the U.S. Army joined our Department of the Navy Knowledge Management Implementation Team for a year and brought along with her recently released information on the former Black program on Remote Viewing, STARGATE. Remote Viewing uses scientific protocol to develop and extend psychic ability to obtain information. It's a pretty rigorous process that requires a team of three. The program had emerged out of the research led by Dr. Robert Monroe, the father of Hemi-Sync®. Several individuals who were involved in the Army's STARGATE program continued to be associated with TMI, even after the founder had passed on.

I never got around to exploring this stuff while working for the Department of the Navy, but after I retired as Chief Knowledge Officer, culminating 20 years of government service, I headed for a week session at TMI. As was to become the pattern when spending a week in meditation at TMI, something wonderful and mysterious happened.

It was early 2002 and as potential buyers we'd been looking at a couple of horses for the farm. One new "neighbor" said he had several geldings that were quite gentle. I decided to try and ride one of them in the ring, clearly a mistake. We were definitely not in sync, and when I inadvertently tightened my right knee he lurched forward. I, on the other hand, bowed backwards over his rear end landing firmly on my head. While David says I was only passed out for a few minutes, then talking to him and saying I was fine, it was about 20 minutes later that I became aware of the situation at hand. One second I'm on a horse riding, the next I'm walking around the grounds looking at a new foal. I asked David, where am I? He quickly caught me up to date on the events of which I had no memory.

My first TMI experience (Gateway) began on Saturday, just a few days after my fall. My head was still aching, and I had pulled something in my lower back, so it was somewhat difficult to walk, and, in particular, to get up and down from a seated position. Still, I was NOT going to waste this opportunity to explore my unconscious!

At night they play some surfing sounds that have Hemi-Sync® beneath them. About half way through the night, I awoke in a fright, with the feeling that I was being pulled down into a vortex, swirling faster and faster, sinking, unable to get out. It took sheer will power to bring myself more fully awake, and then my body was wretching. I ran to the bathroom and sat in misery for 10-15 minutes. My body felt like it was exploding with energy. As things calmed down, I returned to my bedroom. My roommate was awake. "Are you okay?" I didn't know how to respond, and told her what had happened. About a half hour later I decided to try and sleep again. As I started to drift into sleep the vortex was there again; but now it was moving even faster. Down, down, down. No! No! I struggled to pull myself out of the swirling energy, to sit up. I barely made it to the bathroom, wretching, bodily fluids exploding from both ends. Now I was weeping and shaking. The only thought in my head was that I wanted to go home!

My roommate woke the counselor up (who was also a psychologist) and together they coaxed me out of the bathroom. "I'm really sick. I need to go home," I exclaimed. The counselor was a Reiki Master as well. She could feel the energy shooting off of me. She asked if we could sit for a short time and see if we could calm the energy down. She was amazing. I could feel things begin to shift, ever so slowly, and she stayed with me for several hours until the sun rose. Then I dressed and sat through the opening session. By then I was recovering nicely, and realized my head was no longer throbbing.

During the break a young man walked up to me and introduced himself as a Rolfer, that is, a therapist who uses a system of soft tissue manipulation. He said he noticed I was having difficulty getting up and down out of the chairs, and thought he might be able to help. I appreciatively agreed. Within 15 minutes of gentle manipulation, I felt a click and what had been a cutting pain was now a dull soreness, which diminished over the next few days. Yep, you guessed it. I stayed through the entire week, and when David picked me up, I was feeling good and walking well. Since that time I have attended many other sessions at TMI, and something surprising—and wonderful—always happens.

The *Starlines I* program in 2010 was no exception. It was a repeat session for me since I had taken both *Starlines I* and *Starlines II* the previous year. The energy had been so wonderful that I had signed up for both sessions again. A good friend was my roommate, and since I was a repeater the facilitators didn't worry too much about my coming and going to session brief-outs. So once in the energy in my little cubicle, I had the opportunity to stay in it for awhile if I chose. Sure enough, during the first session I went deep, very deep, and was "gone" for two hours! On this inner journey (very much like a dream sequence), I recall meeting David, and the both of us walking through a door into a conference with our "higher counsel." As the door shut behind us, so did my memory shut down. **[At a later date I would recall this, and know that plans were being laid for what was to occur over the next two years.]**

In an evening event later that week, the *Starlines I* group looked at some of the "orb" pictures that a previous group had captured. From the conversation, most of the participants thought of orbs as "spirit orbs." While I was comfortable with this conversation, I didn't really engage at first. What caught my attention was that when I looked closely at one of the orb pictures I could clearly see a human face!

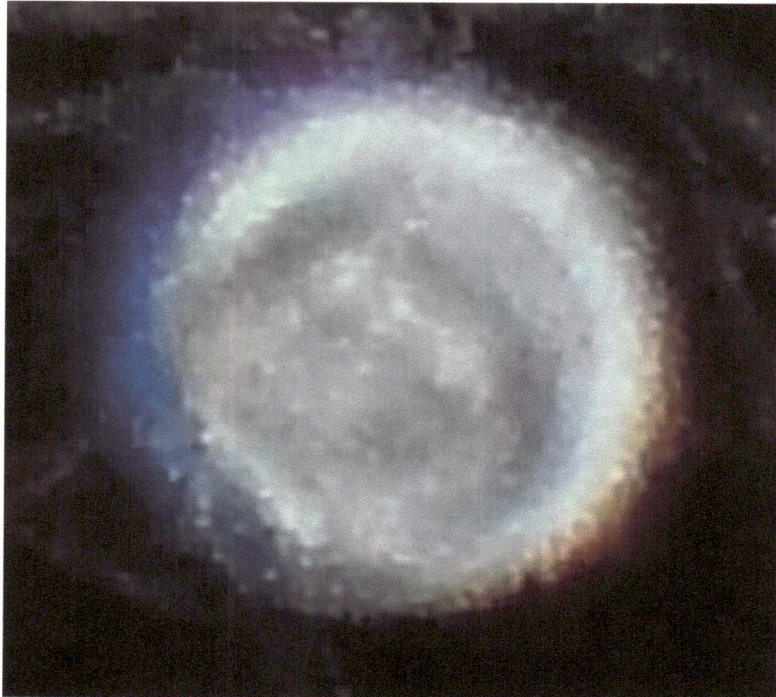

In the first orb picture Alex saw, there appeared to be a face in the orb.

The TMI group agreed to try this orbing. So that evening I joined the group outside in a field at the top of the mountain. In the center is a concrete platform supporting a large crystal. We decided to create a ceremony of sorts to help raise our energy, joining hands and sending love around the circle, then connecting to the larger Universe before calling in the orbs. The experience was fun.

I didn't have a camera with me, but enjoyed feeling the energy and watching the others. I joined in the joyful dancing and singing to call in the orbs. They got some amazing pictures, though none as clear as the one from the previous session, the one with the face. Then, as I looked toward the dark tree line, for a split second I thought I saw a sphere about five feet in diameter, moving just above ground level. I called for someone to take a picture, but then it was gone, although a nearby photographer had some interesting light in the corner of his picture. Was it the orb I had seen, or did the light just bounce-off from his fingers? I knew next time I would have my own camera for the orb pictures. This experience filled me with enough excitement and intrigue to trigger my thoughts about trying to capture orbs at Mountain Quest.

Chapter 3: The Joy of Orbing

Filled with excitement and the promise of something new, something different, something, well, that might head them in new directions, Alex studied the digital cameras in front of her. All the known, well-advertised brands, and others she had never heard of were there, each display model accompanied by a small card broadcasting the intimate details of their innards. As she walked past the displays, she reached her hand out to stroke a Sony Cyber-shot that boasted a 14.1 megapixel capability and included a 10x optical zoom, a 25mm Wide-angle lens, and a red sensor light. David stood quietly behind her, well-versed in her need to "feel" products, connecting to them in a way.

Even before they married, David had been aware of what he described as her "energy sensitivity." Laughing, he remembered that HE had been extremely sensitive to HER energy for months before acknowledging his attraction to her. Both were high energy people, driven to learn and expand. Little wonder the idea of "knowledge" itself had become so paramount in their learning experiences! They were widely published in the areas of Knowledge and Learning.

Alex continued moving around the displays with her hand slightly brushing the cameras, then came back to the Sony Cyber-shot. David recognized the decision-point at play. This camera was the one.

Moving fairly quickly through the generally slow Walmart lines, they headed back to the parking lot. A soft rain played with them as they climbed into the 2002 Jeep Wrangler. Alex settled the package on her lap in the passenger seat, slowly and methodically unwrapping each part of the camera kit. The ride home—an hour-and-a-half through the same two-lane winding country roads as those where the miracle had occurred several months earlier—provided plenty of time to explore the contents.

"What do you think?" David asked.

"Won't really know until I try it out," Alex responded. "But I think one of these options is bound to work!"

Indeed, there were several options that *might* work, the "Easy Shooting" and just maybe the "Intelligent Auto Adjustment." The movie and sweep panorama were interesting, but not the current focus. The manual and program modes were interesting, but how could she set a distance when she didn't know exactly where—or even what—she was shooting? There was also a scene selection mode, but that carried with it the same difficulties. David wondered, what WAS she planning to shoot?

Darkness was settling across the farm as they drove down the long drive and around behind the house. But the rain had stopped and stars were popping out above, happy to share their freedom of light. Alex hopped out, "I'm going to go out and try my new camera," she announced.

"See you later," David responded, smiling. That was his girl! Always eager to explore something new. Truth be told, the orb picture she had shown him had sparked some interest in him as well. He could see the two eyes and nose of the face she described within the yellow-orange orb. He made a mental note that he needed to take the time to explore the origin of these pictures. Water? Dust? Electromagnetic energy? Possibly all that, and maybe more. He would search the Internet and scan Amazon offerings related to orbs. That would serve as a starting place. There was certainly a natural explanation for the picture. But for now, he would lay down and take a nap for a short while. Still recovering from his brush with death, his energy had been depleted by the trip to Walmart. Exploration of the orb phenomenon would have to wait until tomorrow.

10 | P a g e

Alex had been aching to try out the camera. Her heart was bubbling with joy and expectation. Above she could see part of the Milky Way galaxy splashing across the clear night sky, amazing clouds that were not clouds but a collection of so many stars and systems, no doubt accented by gases. There were no lights below to distract from the beauty of this panorama. She twirled a couple of times, cramping her neck to scan the wide expanse above for a chance glimpse of a shooting star. There was one! "Thank you, Universe," she sang out, then continued singing her request, "Orbs of light, come into my picture please tonight."

She circled around the farmhouse in the darkness, which now was punctuated regularly by flashes of light from the camera. When she found a spot that felt right, she stayed there for a while. And sure enough, there were small circles and dots across the viewing screen of her camera, roundly punctuating the white field fence, the dark leaves and trees, the even darker mountains. The night was fruitful.

Alex saw small circles and dots across the viewing screen of her camera, roundly punctuating the white field fence.

When the chill dictated it was time to go inside, she pulled the pictures up on her computer, a Sony Vaio. She would crop all of the orbs, enlarge them, compare them, and categorize them. This process would repeat itself every night throughout the summer. As her collection of orbs reached into the thousands and continued expanding, she enjoyed the amazing variety of size, color, density and patterns.

Alex noted similarities as well. For example, when she would blow up the bright white ones, they would appear to have the opposite colors of the spectrum on each side, recalling the color nemonic Roy-G-Biv. She was able to pick out the red-orange-yellow on one side and the blue-indigo-violet on the other. Occasionally she would also see green somewhere in the middle!

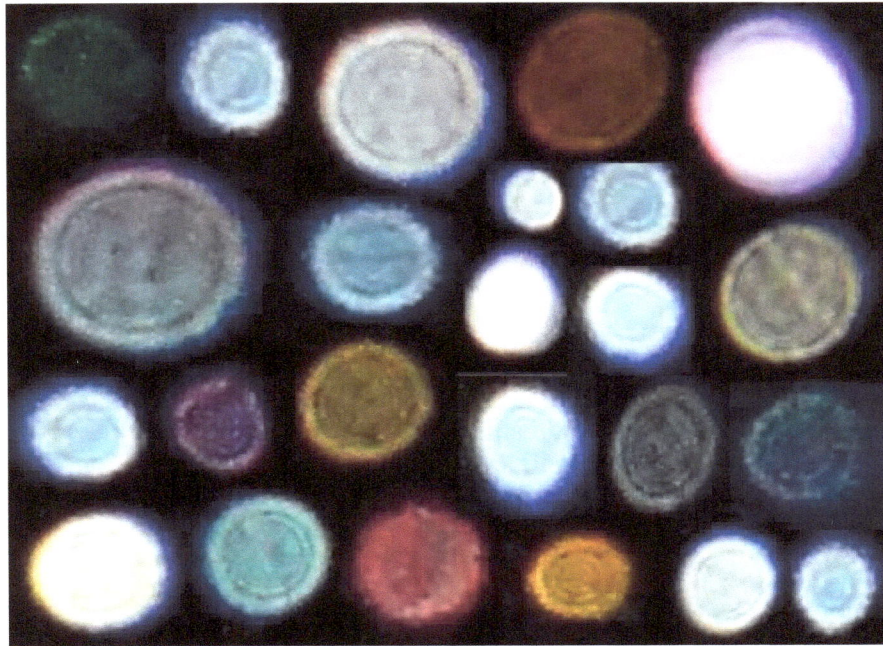

A collage of orbs (captured in different pictures), pieced together to show the variety of size, color, density and patterns.

ROY-G-BIVs
(Red-Orange-Yellow-Green-Blue-Indigo-Violet)

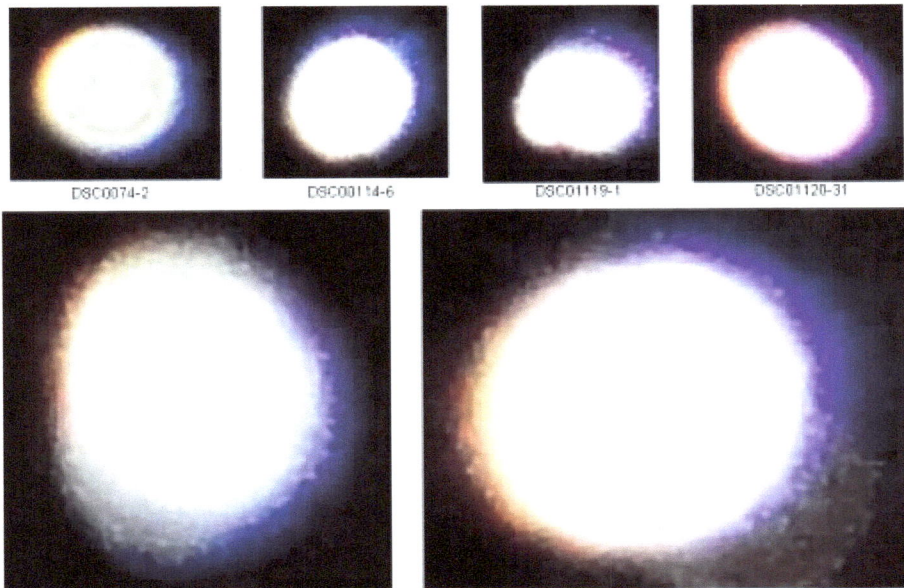

These Roy-G-Biv orb pictures were taken at different times.

Sometimes the Roy-G-Biv's would move so fast that they made a streak of light in the camera. Yet you could still see the color shifts.

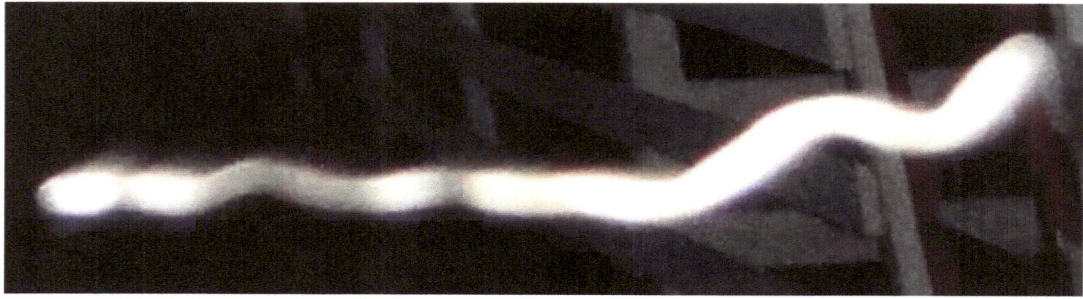

At the left you can see the orb shapes. The Roy-G-Biv orbs appear to have a higher level of energy. Was this one orb moving fast or multiple orbs?

One night in late July, Alex discovered a beautiful red orb in a large maple tree at the back of the complex. Below the spreading limbs sat a 2-foot half-round rock carved and painted with the words "The Knowledge Tree". The orb was about half-way up the tree, as red as any orb she had ever caught in the camera. The next evening as she was circling the complex, she stopped to reflect on that red orb. She shot a picture of the tree, but there were no orbs. "Sure wish I could see that red orb again!" she sang, and took another picture. Sure enough, clear and beautiful, there was a red orb in the middle of the tree. This was Alex's first recognition that she was "calling in" the orbs.

Alex was excited when the red orb appeared in the same general location where it had been previously photographed.

Prior to going outside the following evening, Alex told David about her experience with the red orb. "Interesting coincidence," David responded. She nodded and, with a twinkle in her eye, invited David to join her for her evening orbing experience.

"Maybe we can confirm that coincidence" she teased. Alex grabbed David's hand, guiding him out the front door and down two steps to the front walk. David's eyes were slower in adjusting to the dark, although with a nearly full moon this evening and sky full of stars it didn't take long. Alex began to sing as they circled around to The Knowledge Tree (a towering old maple situated at a rear corner of the retreat center), occasionally shooting a picture along the way. They stopped right in front of the tree. "Why don't you stand there so I can get you in the picture as well," Alex suggested.

"Okay," David agreed. He had no expectations, but enjoyed their interactions when he occasionally walked out to see how her orbing was going. He did marvel at the variety of orbs in her pictures and had begun to try to explore what was, in fact, going on. Still, he had no expectations for this picture.

Alex shot a picture of the tree, and there was no red orb, indeed, no orbs at all. She showed the picture to David. "Look, there are no orbs," she stated.

"I see that," he affirmed.

Alex looked at him and stepped back a few feet. "We'll take another," she smiled. She began to sing: "Orbs of night, beautiful orbs of light, come into my picture tonight. So beautiful the color red, come out and show yourself tonight, beautiful orb of light."

As she repeated the first line, she raised her camera and shot a picture.

"Well?" David chided.

"Well," Alex responded, "another coincidence."

She pulled up the picture on the camera screen and showed it to him. "Hmm," David hummed. "This certainly bears more exploration."

Alex:

I went out every night to capture orbs in my camera. It was fun, and the exercise filled me with joy. Along the way I began to observe intelligent behavior, so I talked to the orbs, and then began to sing to them as my heart became involved more fully in the wonderful evening romps. As I sang and danced there were more and more orbs in my pictures. And they were listening to me! At the end of one evening I noted (in my song) that I had not seen any blue orbs. As I sang goodbye and took my last camera shot, there was an array of blue orbs!

When Alex asked for blue orbs a plethora of blue orbs appeared.

Then things became even *more* interesting. One night I was out with the horses shooting away. There are always orbs near animals. I wanted to get a shot of our beautiful Arabian Mystical Quest, one of the youngsters born here on the farm whom we love oh so much. Every time I came close enough to take a shot, Mystical would move toward me to get scratched and petted. The third time she started my direction I called out, "Mystical I love you, but *please* stay still!" She hesitated long enough for me to get the picture. And when I blew that picture up, there was an orb in the shape of a heart moving toward her side!

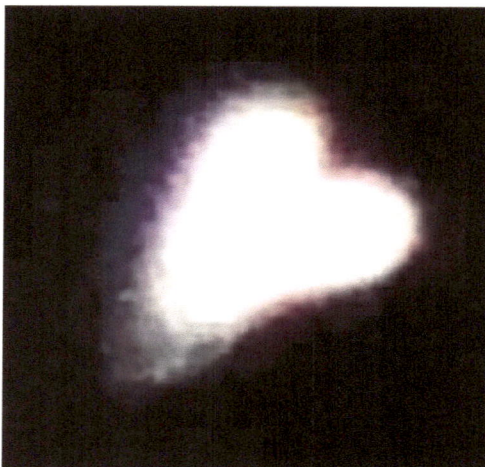

When Alex enlarged that picture, a heart-shaped orb was flying into Mystical's side.

A wedding at Mountain Quest was planned for the middle of August. The bride and groom were an older couple. The couches in the library were moved out to make way for a DJ and dance floor. The groom was so happy! He laughed and danced and the group partied for hours. From the second floor of the library Alex peered down through the guard rails and shot a few pictures. Each picture showed one or more orbs around the groom, sometimes attached to him, other times appearing to be dancing with him! And orbs were floating all around outside the facility. This experience reaffirmed what Alex was beginning to understand, that the orbs appeared to be attracted to higher-order energies such as love and joy.

Orbs were floating around outside the facility.

A few days later Alex had the opportunity to again confirm this. As she went about her orbing, a couple who were staying at the Inn asked her what she was doing. "Orbing," came the response. They asked what that was. "Orbs can be specks of dust, or little drops of mist, or they can be electromagnetic energy, all of which I find fascinating!"

Alex showed the couple a few pictures she had taken. They were amazed. "Can you get a picture of us with orbs?"

Alex smiled. "If you can feel love and joy I can. You see, these wonderful, strange spheres of energy seem to be attracted to love and joy. I only get pictures of them when I am feeling that way." So the couple began to tell each other jokes, tickle each other, play. And after a few minutes, the playing wasn't just being acted, it was real, and the laughter began to emerge. That is when the orbs came into the picture. Alex watched as the transformation occurred. Alex thought, "It really *doesn't* matter what the orbs are made of … if the process of orbing can make people happy, then there needs to be more orbing in the world!" To help keep the memory of this joyful experience alive for the couple, Alex printed a copy of the best picture for them to take home.

There was another couple that came to the Inn for a one-day honeymoon. They were down-to-earth people who had been childhood sweethearts and after many years had come back together. That was a beautiful story to Alex. Camera in hand, she went about trying to help them document their special visit to the Inn. When Alex shot a picture as they came through the family room in the house, there were orbs in the picture! And a bunch of small orbs had come together to create what looked like a lovebird, right over the newly-weds' heads.

A bunch of small orbs came together to create a lovebird.

Karen:

Ron and I grew up together and went through middle school and high school together. When we graduated we each went our separate way, married, raised kids, and later each of us divorced. Over 30 years following our youthful romance, we met back up and fell in love all over again. We spent our wedding night at the Inn at Mountain Quest.

When Alex showed us to our room, she had a camera in her hand, and asked if we would like to have a picture or two to remember this special night. We thought that was a great idea, and she took several shots of us in our Quest Room. Then, as we were walking down through the family room outside the kitchen, Alex took another picture of us. There in the picture, above Ron's head, was a large orb. And above us appeared a form made up of several orbs that looked like a lovebird, or even an angel! It was an amazing experience to see an orb for the first time, and to see the orbs come together to create such a beautiful sight for us. It certainly has caught our attention! The radiant love from an angel! We treasure that photograph.

David:

I think it was because of the possible intelligent behavior that Alex was experiencing with the orbs— juxtaposed with the fact that so many people on the Internet believed that the orbs were only a reflection of dust in front of the camera—that I became curious about what they really were. It is always easier to accept simplistic answers instead of having to study an unusual phenomenon or, worse yet, having to change one's belief system.

As Alex kept getting more and more pictures of orbs and observing more and more responsive behaviors, I began to ask myself questions about the physical conditions (temperature, wind, humidity, barometric pressure) and what, if any, were the social and emotional conditions of the photographer or people who are being photographed which might affect the chances of capturing orbs on a given night? It appears that the orbs find a more **joyful and positive environment** attractive, and—as we would expect— wind and water do affect the behavior of the orbs.

Hmmm. How could the joyful, positive attitude of humans have an effect on electromagnetic spheres? What are the orbs, really? Or are we just deluding ourselves. Just because "we" get happy and feel good when we see orbs does not imply that the orbs are there because we are happy. I was not sure how much professional research had gone into understanding the relationship among orbs, the local environment and humans.

If there is a connecting relationship between orbs and humans, then in my rational mind it almost has to be gravitational, acoustic or electromagnetic. Of these, the electromagnetic field seems to be the most likely, and we know individuals can and do radiate and receive low levels of the electromagnetic field. We do know that each of us can sense when another person appears, feels or behaves in a happy manner. If there *does* exist an influential relationship between orbs and human happiness, can we understand it from science or from spirituality, or perhaps a combination of the two? When we move from the known to the unknown we must be very careful not to demand that the explanations of the unknowns be similar to the explanations we have learned that explain the knowns of our current knowledge.

Where they are discussed, there is considerable controversy over the source of orbs. The American Heritage Dictionary says that orbs are spheres or spherical objects. The Wikipedia says that the term orb describes unexpected, typically circular artifacts that occur in flash photography—sometimes with trails indicating motion—especially common with modern compact and ultra compact digital cameras. As with many phenomena that are unusual, there are those that firmly believe that orbs are created solely by dust, pollen, water droplets, and/or other solid particles close to, and in front of, the camera lens. This is the standard materialist interpretation and position, and under some circumstances this can occur. However, there is also a spiritual or paranormal perspective that orbs are electromagnetic spheres of various sizes.

Alex had taken a large number of orb pictures ranging from single orbs to dozens in the same picture. When observed closely, many of the orbs had faces in them, most often taking the appearance of animals (which certain makes sense because we live on a farm), and came in a wide variety of colors. It is difficult to see how a dust particle could reflect such a range of colors. It is also difficult to perceive seeing only one particle of dust in front of a camera since dust usually comes with many, many particles moving around together. Further, why would they be in one picture, and then not in the next, and then mysteriously appear again several pictures later?

One hunch Alex had was this was somehow related to the way the picture-taker—and the people in the picture—felt. Alex had found that when people were joyful and happy the chances of orbs around them or nearby was high. Alex had also found that orbs were almost always around animals and children.

Ella (the Llama) and her pet sheep Clover sit quietly as guests invite the orbs into the picture.
Orbs are almost always around animals and children.

Becoming more interested in this borderline phenomena between science and spirituality, I reviewed other web articles and several books on orbs and orbing. It's unusual for me to read materials on the Internet, since I'm admittedly of the old school in terms of research. Still, there seem to be two camps. Many web articles on orbs were certain that they were caused by dust particles or camera malfunctions. It was the old yes-no, right-wrong, good-bad, either-or type of thinking that blocks learning but simplifies the complexity of the world and reduces our fear of the unknown by simply believing it does not exist.

There also were several articles (and several books) that recognize the reality of orbs as something different, perhaps spirit orbs, and some even considered the conditions that encouraged orbs to appear. These conditions were similar to what Alex has already described. From a physics viewpoint, I perceive orbs as basically electromagnetic spheres that can move quickly, but most likely not at the speed of light. The many colors they possess are explained by the electrons in the atoms of the orb that have been energized by the camera's flash. The flash energy moves the electrons to a higher energy level and then very quickly they decay, resulting in a specific color being radiated as the electron gives off energy during its passage to the ground level of the atom. Since the camera's flash excites electrons in the orb to different energy levels, when they fall back to ground state they radiate different frequencies (colors), which also can create the Roy-G-Biv spectrum mentioned earlier. There are probably other physics phenomena going on as well. I needed to investigate this further.

Chapter 4: October 4, 2010

The night was quite dark. A few stars were peeking into the blackness that surrounded Alex as she stepped carefully down the two steps of the front porch and the short brick walk to the driveway. There was a soft meow to the right. Clearly Cat Walker, her feral friend, had either calculated or sensed her arrival time. As Alex leaned over and picked up the heavy cat she caught the soft smell of hay and felt his still-warm fur. On cool nights he slept in the hayloft. Alex wondered, "How did he do it? How did he know just the right time to arrive at the front walk for his nightly hug?" And as Cat Walker headed her way he always seemed to be trailing orbs.

Catwalker always seemed to be trailing orbs.
(Pictures at the top are enlarged replicas of the orbs in the lower picture.)

With the cat snuggled against her chest, Alex walked a short way down the drive, singing quietly, then clicked her first picture of the night. There was a small green orb showing bright against a backdrop of orange, yellow, red and some still-green leaves. Later she would note the dark rings within the green orb, and the faint shape of two eyes, two ears and the long nose of a dog, an orb that often appeared in her pictures and which she perceived as a representation of her precious Sashi, an Akita who had passed the previous January.

In the distance, some half mile away, a truck moved along the road in front of the farm, a soft rise and fall of vibration punctuating the coming and going. Alex swung around 180 degrees and took a second shot, then took another of the mini-horse field, now to her right. Nothing of consequence, but she kept singing, a smile on her face. Heading her original direction, she took another shot. There were several orbs in this one, tiny flecks of light with specks of green and blue, not quite as well defined as the first. Passing the white fence of the Llama pen, she turned toward the Retreat Center for her next shot. There were several orbs, only she must have moved the camera. They seemed a bit fuzzy on the camera screen.

Talking to herself, mostly through lilting melodies, she sang: "Orbs of light, beautiful energies of the night, show yourself for me tonight." While the tones stopped, the words continued in a conversational tone: "My friends of light, I need more. My husband David is a skeptic [in repeating this story later this word would be changed to "scientist" since David prefers not to be called a "skeptic"] and, well, I just need more evidence of your intelligence. Could you perhaps shape an animal for me to capture in my picture?" Laughing, she swung around toward the Llama pen and took a photograph of Pixar, a white Llama sitting peacefully on the ground.

Smiling, Alex quickly looked at the screen, then caught her breath as the camera clicked back into photo mode. Had she really seen what she thought she had? She pulled her glove off and pressed the access button, waiting, waiting, waiting. Then the photo was there, hundreds of connected orbs gracefully arching above the sitting Pixar.

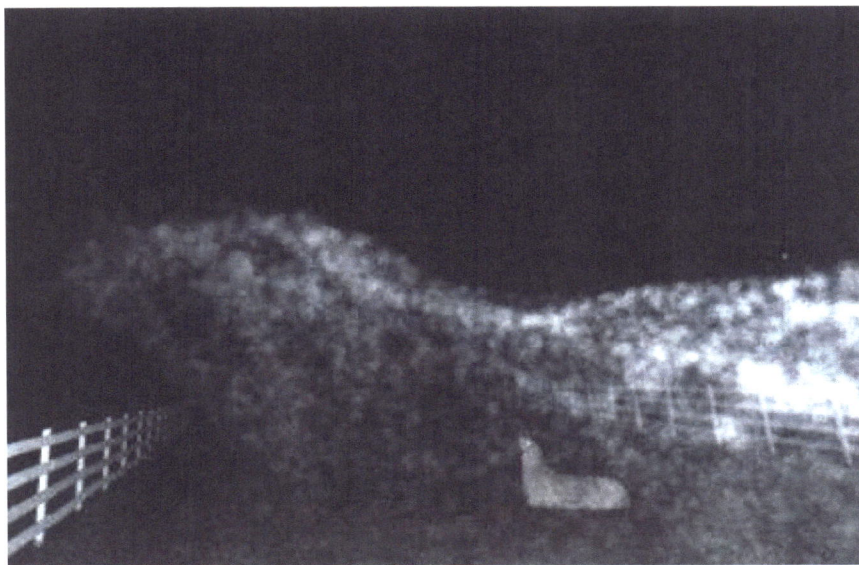

There above Pixar, our white Llama sitting on the ground,
were several hundred orbs taking the shape of a large Llama!

"David!" She banged through the front door and quickly navigated the stairs to their living rooms at the top of the old farmhouse. David sat in his office reading. "Look at this!"

They moved together into Alex's office, with Alex diving into the seat in front of the computer and quickly uploading to the larger computer screen the photograph she had just taken. They both stood mesmerized. Alex slowly enlarged an area over to the right that appeared a bit brighter. Faces? Yep, the sense of two eyes in spheres and soft marks that expressed other features. Were they making this up? But there it was on the computer, with clear, distinct lines mimicking the lines of Pixar sitting on the ground below.

David

I looked at the back of the camera, and at first saw only two outlines of what appeared to be animals. After focusing in on the bottom animal, it was clearly our Llama—probably Pixar—the one with the white coat of hair. A much larger pattern hovered over Pixar, and looked like the long neck and mid body of a Llama about 10 to 20 times the size of Pixar. Two questions immediately came to my mind: Was the small one really Pixar? And where did the large one come from?

After telling me her story of asking for some validation, we both wanted to print a much larger sized picture so we could study it more carefully. From my reading of the work by Dr. Klaus Heinemann and others, I had begun to think of orbs as electromagnetic spherical shells. As such the orbs could not form a smooth surface, unless they were to become so small that together they appeared continuous to the human eye. I would question this latter thought when the *Myst* appeared.

After studying an 8x10 sized photo, I was able to clearly see the resemblance between Pixar and the pattern of the orbs. The upper, larger pattern of the orbs looked like a Llama stretching its neck. Clearly it is not a precise outline of a large Llama; on the other hand, is the resemblance accidental? Or could it be due to what the observer wanted to see, without even realizing it? As a scientist, I like to think that I can be very objective when I feel it's the best way to go. Certainly, the Llama picture offered many subjective interpretations. We all seem to have a tendency to see what is on our minds at the time, or what we would like to see, and often see what we believe to be true. Thus, the picture could (or possibly should?) be dismissed as a self-made prophecy. After some thought, I think **not**.

We knew that the bottom pattern in the camera was, and still is, a real Llama. He was in front of Alex. We feed him every day, we talk to him and we pet him. And we know that the larger pattern above Pixar is not something material in nature that we can touch, pet and feed. So, are we hallucinating or seeing something that is not there? While we know that the upper pattern is not a "real" Llama, the question is, does the pattern provide an answer to Alex's question for evidence of the orb's intelligence by shaping an animal for her?

From a materialist perspective the picture does not prove that the orbs deliberately formed the pattern in answer to Alex's request. This picture/phenomenon has not been repeated, although other similar situations *have* occurred (which is shared in volume 2 of our journey, *Patterns in the Myst*). Yet, of all possible patterns that could be formed by orbs, the one that came into being at that particular time was amazingly like a large Llama. Why? Was it random? Certainly, the fence, and Pixar, both in the picture, were not random. They would be there if anyone had taken a picture at this time and place. But what about the orbs? If they were random, it seems that they would have been *scattered* throughout the picture, or perhaps not in the picture at all. Yet they *were* in the picture, and the outline clearly resembles that of a large Llama, at the specific moment in time after Alex had asked for some evidence. Coincidence? Possible, but highly improbable. While we can never be certain of the interpretation of our observations, to both Alex and I there was sufficient evidence to excite our interest and imply possibilities beyond our usual materialist focus. This phenomenon was gently pulling us into a world that I had never spent much time thinking about. Although Alex was much closer to this "spiritual world" than I was, I was determined to keep an open mind and see where it would take us.

I recognized years ago that science continuously learns, updates that learning, and changes its understanding of phenomena. In other words, no knowledge is absolute. Many things we take for granted today were paranormal a hundred years ago. An open mind looks for possibilities, probabilities, evidence and explanations whenever faced with a "coincidence" or anomaly.

Clearly, we needed to learn more about the phenomena of orbs and their relationships to our/their environment. It amazes me to think that Alex and a large number of electromagnetic spheres are really communicating in any manner. I thought of Shakespeare's line in Hamlet: "There are more things in Heaven and Earth, Horatio, than are dreamed of in your philosophy." Indeed, Shakespeare was brilliant. The more we know, the more we recognize that what we do not know will always be larger than what we know. This is a challenge to humanity.

Alex and I talked about the occurrence and knew that we were going to be on the lookout for other incidents or coincidences regarding Alex, orbs and the local situation and environment. In our research here at Mountain Quest, our knowledge, learning, organizational design and leadership studies have indicated there is no substantial conflict (and perhaps a great deal of synergism and insights to be learned) among science, spirituality and humanism. This encounter with the orbs gave us the fascinating opportunity to learn more about these three pillars of our world.

The day after seeing the orbs formed and shaped above the Llama Pixar, Alex couldn't wait for night to fall. There was tremendous excitement in every inch of her body as she tore out the front door and went to exactly the same spot she'd stood the night before when she caught the first "*Myst*" form. She watched the last rays of the sun fade over the top of the western mountain range, and the soft evening glows damper with darkness as beautiful pin points began to emerge in the blanket of darkness. It was a clear night. What would she see tonight? Her expectations were expanding with her imagination.

Taking a deep breath and trying very hard to stay calm, she began to sing with a soft and soothing voice, asking the orbs to form and shape for her camera, for her. A few orbs appeared in her first picture. She continued, undaunted. Another orb or two. She tried again and again throughout the evening, happy with the orbs, but now beginning to question whether she would be able to repeat the picture of yesterday. She looked at the stars and tried to imagine them coming down, tried to imagine reaching out and touching them. She felt like she could touch them.

Alex kept asking, but there was nothing in her picture. Thoughts kept running through her mind. "I made this up." "This is my imagination." "It won't happen again." "Perhaps it was an accident." As disappointment softly welled up inside, she stayed persistent, singing and shooting, moving in a circle to check all around her, pointing straight up (just in case). Nothing now, not even orbs.

"Perhaps it is me," she pondered. What am I doing wrong? Not feeling enough joy? She tried to bolster her joy level, remembering their miracle, feeling the love for their animals, admiring the beauty of the Milky Way, breathing in the cool air and the smells of the farm.

Finally, with fingers beginning to numb, Alex called it a night and went to bed. Snuggling in the warm flannel sheets, she reflected on the amazing phenomenon of the orbs, visioning the picture from the previous day, and re-membering how the orbs had come together to form and shape a Llama. ***She wanted more***.

Alex

Funny how human beings are never happy with what they have, isn't it? Something amazing happens, and then we question whether it is real or not. Something even more amazing happens, and we want it to happen again and again to make sure we're not imagining it.

But it's more than that. (There is that darn "more" word again!) We WANT more. There are things that I've REALLY wanted in my life, and I've worked hard to get them. Then, somewhere along the path to getting them, they seem to lose their importance, because once I have them they aren't so important and there is *something else* that becomes more important. Hmmm.

In my belief set we are all connected, all part of a Oneness of larger energy and love of which I am comfortable using the term God to describe. As a very tiny part of this Oneness, this magnificent power of the Universe, I have a unique point of view. David and I often remind ourselves that every single human being is different than any other human being that ever has been or ever will be … while there appear to be similarities in the "models" of humans, there are so many differences in the experience of each human. The illusion of separation gives us this wonderful opportunity of differentiating, and observing the "other" from a unique subjective viewpoint. And as we create our thoughts and feelings about that which is *not perceived as "I"*, we are expanding all that is, what I call God's thought.

Have I pushed too much into a few sentences? The idea is that as small as we are, as large as we are, we (all of us) are on the front edge of discovery and learning. It's similar to the way our mind works. Our mind/brain is an associative patterner. All the new stuff coming in through all of our senses is combined with the stuff we've stored in various parts of our brain and body. So we are continuously creating the NOW specifically for the moment at hand, it's always new, we are always expanding.

Understand that a single thought may be stored in many different places in the brain, touching a thousand, a million or even more neurons. Come people liken the mind to a computer, but it's nothing like a computer! Well, that's too blunt a statement … perhaps it would be similar to a biological computer if there were such a thing (and no doubt that will become a reality sooner than we think!) But back to the mind/brain. The way we store information is not through groups of words to form phrases, sentences and paragraphs. We only store the *most significant* parts of information in our memory, the things that seem the most important. How do we determine what is most significant or important? Well, one sure way is through emotion. Those things we have strong emotions about have stronger connections, and many more connections, than those things to which we pay little or no attention.

Now all this is off the top of my head, without referencing (or having David check my words), and without the context to help you fully understand the intent of what I am saying. So I apologize if I am leaving some pertinent information out. Of course, this is the exact way the mind/brain works, what I'm trying to describe. The things that are the *most important* to me are the things that come up when I share a stream of consciousness like this one!

The bottom line is that *what I had experienced with the orbs was not enough.* I wanted more. I wanted to see more. I wanted to understand more.

What would happen next?

Chapter 5: Then the Angels Came

Alex got the "more" she wanted ... in fact, much "more" than she ever expected.

It was October 6, 2010, two days after the orbs formed and shaped a huge Llama above the Mountain Quest Llama Pixar. Alex decided to do her meditation before going outside that evening. The meditation Alex repeated every evening before going to bed had emerged over the course of ten years, and no matter how she felt or how tired she was, she made sure to move through this meditation. Alex would not go to bed until it was done. She guessed meditating every night was part of that responsibility thing she felt, and, yes, meditating DID make her feel better. In this evening ritual Alex would release any negative stuff that had connected itself to her during the day, fill all of her bodies with love and light, and surround herself with light. When she finished this process, she always felt a sense of well-being—safe and filled with love, and happy. And since the orbs were always there right away when Alex felt happy, it just made sense to go out orbing AFTER she completed her meditation. At least she decided to try it out. [Alex's Meditation is in Appendix A.]

When she finally went out with her camera, Alex was calmer than the previous night, floating with contentment and happiness, although this was seasoned with a bit of anticipation. Her first shot was a picture of several hundred orbs towering about 40 feet reaching from the small garden in front of the Inn. While faded because of the distance and blackness of the night, in the picture there were lots of orbs visibly rising above the fountain. In the second shot, approximately 4.5 seconds later, the orbs moved toward her, covering perhaps half the distance, and now rose only about 20 feet into the air. "This is great" Alex thought, smiling.

On the first shot orbs stretched for about 40 feet above the
small garden and fountain; on the second they were closer.

In the light of the flash from her third shot, approximately 4.5 seconds later, Alex saw with her eyes a pink apparition looming about 15 feet above her and about 7 feet off to the left. The figure's pink face was bony, and it looked like there was a mirror image of the face coming off from the back of the head. The torso could have been that of a barrel-chested skeleton, only it was pink, like the head, not the faded white of Halloween visitors. There were no legs, just a slight blur of pink where the legs would have been, but the outline of wings protruded on both sides. Prone to imagining, Alex would have thought this figure was her imagination, but in the darkness of the night the pink shape dominated the picture on her camera screen as well!

At first Alex thought she was imagining what she thought she saw;
but then there it was in her picture.

Alex's thoughts were racing. Wings. Could this be an angel? Only that pink bony face registered in her brain as "scary." And seeing this character with her own eyes had given her a start … that was quite different than something showing up on the camera screen! Now it's hard to say whether Alex spoke out loud or in her mind, but her question was clear: "Should I be afraid?" Instantly, something touched her left shoulder. It felt like a hand, the pressure of palm and lightness of fingers. And waves of love washed through her, over her. Sighing, accepting, happy, Alex responded, this time undoubtedly out loud, "That's good enough for me!" And she just kept on shooting pictures.

Alex's October 6 Journal Entry

Photographs DSC05659-05819. Returned to spot where I had caught the llama "grouping" and no luck. But kept shooting (getting some orbs) and then caught a large number of orbs coming from behind the bush in the garden area (up to about 40 feet) (DSC05726). Then they separated into smaller faded groups and headed my way (DSC05727). In DSC05728 you can see some sort of shape emerging in the center of the picture … while it appears to be in the garden, it is closer to me. In DSC05729 only a few orbs. Then in DSC05730 a "spector", large (although not as large as it appears because it is much closer), maybe four feet above my head to the left and five feet in front of me. It had a pinkish glow and the shape was human-like … I immediately thought of the Archangel Michael (warrior). When this picture occurred, since it was off to the left and my camera was in my right hand, I actually caught the vision in my own eyes. There was a moment of realization that I could catch this stuff with my eyes when the camera flash went off. It was also a moment where I asked myself: "Should I be afraid?" Immediately I felt a pressure on my left shoulder accompanied by an incredible flow of love passing through me. Clearly the answer was "no." So, I lowered the camera to my right shoulder and kept shooting, looking now in front of the camera as the flash went off so I could see what was there with my own eyes. (Maybe 20 seconds between 05730 and 05731.)

Now in DSC05731 several of what I call "furies" came through from the left. They were quite beautiful, triangle shapes with the pointed head at the right, winged with face, or what I believed were faces but they moved through so fast with a short flash time that I really couldn't make out any particulars.

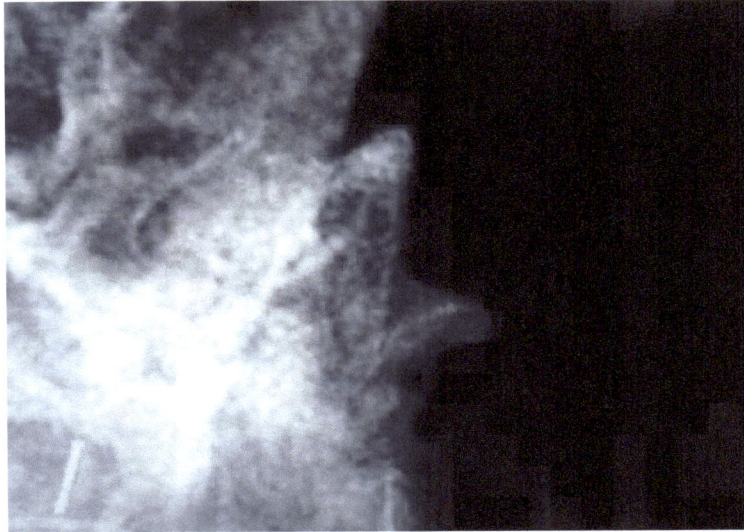

Then beautiful, triangle shapes moved in from the left.

Another blank, then in DSC05734 there is a large character to my upper right (not caught other than a piece of it), then in DSC0575, moving in from the left. Then in DSC05736 there were several small "angels" with a "vortex" opening behind them. These are reflected in the picture.

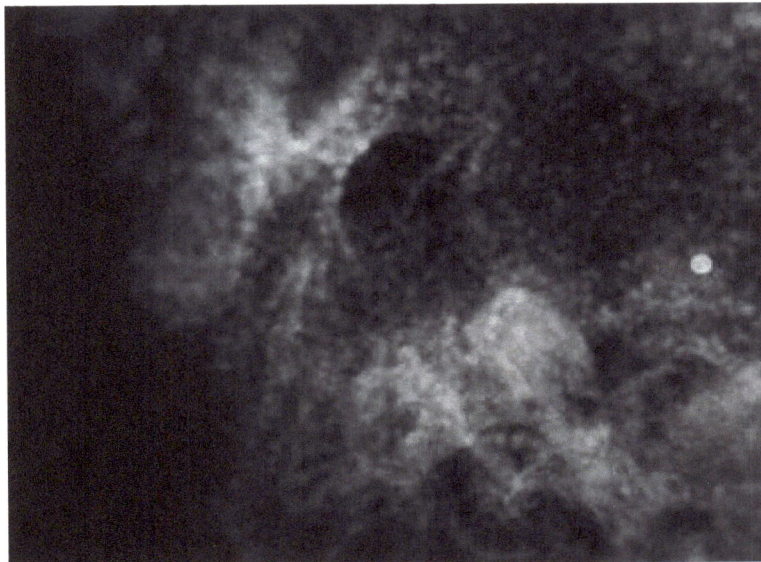

Alex wondered, "Could this be a wormhole? Or is my imagination getting the best of me!"

(Could this be the end of a wormhole? Or is my imagination getting the best of me!) I was quite excited, so began to dance a step or two. Almost humorously, there were curly ribbons of orbs in the next shot. Then two shots later a large object with wings flew in from the left (DSC05739).

NOTE: It appears that all of these objects are made of the same energy as the orbs, having both large "whole" appearances and, when blown up, showing some orbs with specific characteristics. All together there were well over 20 wonderful pictures, each quite different than the next.

* * * * *

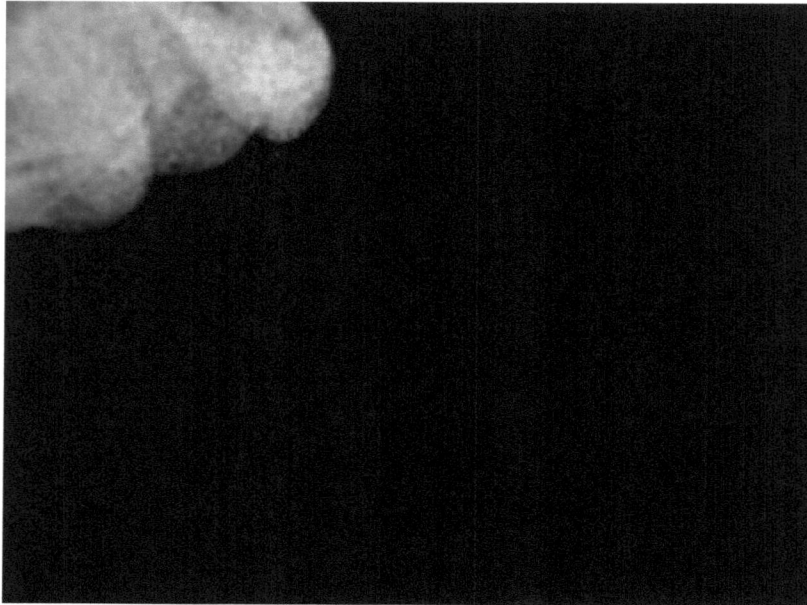

When a large object with wings flew in from the left, Alex caught one wing in her picture.

After these initial experiences a large part of Alex's "days" were devoted to exploring the pictures from the previous night, and her nights were full of joyfully playing with the *Myst*. She would go out when darkness fell, in the middle of the night, and before sunrise. David was wonderfully supportive. She began to move around the fields near the house to see if she could capture in different places what at that point she could only think of as "plasma." At first the phenomenon was often of enormous proportions, everywhere around her and above her. Alex was ecstatic! But when she looked at those pictures, there was no definition, no way that anyone else could tell what was happening. Alex said to the visitors, "If this is for me, you've got me. It's wonderful! But if I'm to share this with anyone, or explore the patterns, there needs to be some boundaries, some form and shape." So, the "visitors" began to form and shape about two feet in front of her and brought their size down to generally under two feet. Now Alex could capture the shapes of the *Myst* in her camera.

When she was getting ready to go back inside, Alex would tell her visitors that she was leaving and provide some detail such as "My fingers are cold" or "The battery is low" or "It's time to go to bed." The shapes of light would appear one more time, and then be gone … unless she called them back, which she often did to say one more goodnight as she reached the porch.

On October 10, 2010, at the end of the first week of this new routine, Alex was shooting in the back field in front of the rising mountains, although the night was so dark that the backdrop of her pictures just appeared black. Moved to tears with the beauty of the shapes forming before her responding to her singing, she began to ask the questions that had been welling up inside. She sang, "Beautiful angels in the sky, beautiful angels tell me why … Help me learn and help me grow, I want to see what I can know …." After a chorus or two sending love and light, she asked, "What is my purpose, why am I here?" Unable to quickly think of a rhyme, she went on with a chorus of "Beautiful angels …."

After the question was asked Alex saw the formed plasma in her camera light, but had to look closely at the picture to figure out what was there. Sure enough, there was an answer! She could see a figure of light with outstretched arms while a darker form loomed above. The brightest spot of light was coming from the chest of the figure, in the vicinity of the heart. Several other forms of light were supporting from the rear. Alex quickly recognized the answer to her question: "We are here bringing light into the world!"

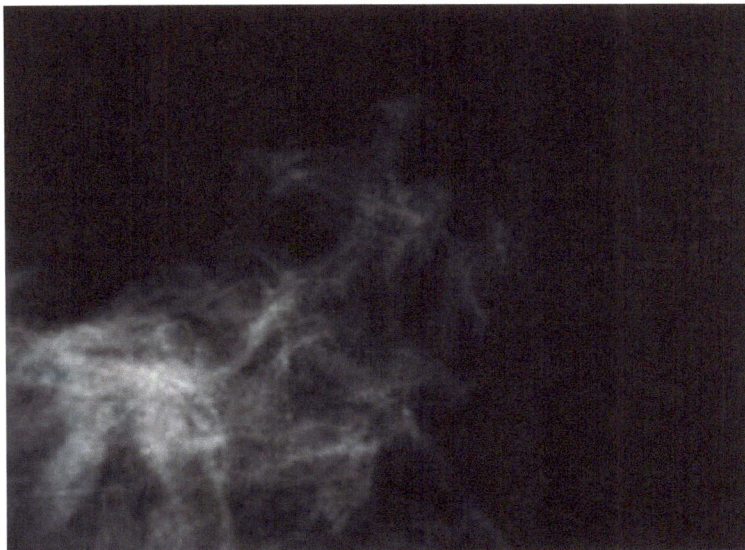

Supported from behind, Alex could see a figure of light with outstretched arms while a darker form loomed above.

Delighted, Alex continued to ask questions and continued to get pictures in response, although admittedly some of them were difficult to figure out at first, and would only later make any sense. But others were immediately recognizable. There was an angel, with wings open, looking down at her! When she was to blow this up on the computer screen, there were layers of faces embedded throughout the wings, a single orb above the angel's head, and the appearance of so many other orbs making up the larger shape.

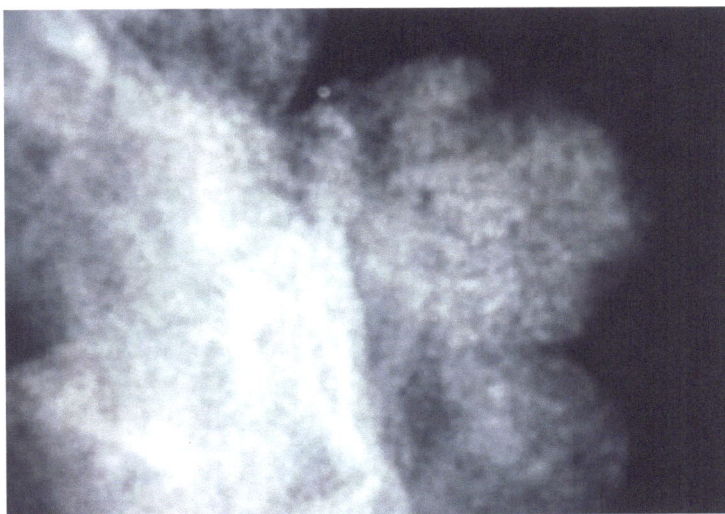

The Myst angel's wings were outstretched, and a single orb was above her head.

Alex:

In tears, not daring to believe this interaction was truly occurring, I asked if my father was present when my mother passed. He had died more than ten years before my mother's passing. And there in the picture appeared the face of my father, rounded with medium light hair, a bit longer than he wore it, now a winged figure holding in his arms a seated woman with darker hair wearing a plaid coat with a fur collar. There was a scattering of pink throughout the coat. My mother had such a coat, one of those 1950's specials that were like a car coat in length, plaid blue and pink with a fake fur collar.

There was my mother seated in my father's arms. My mind quickly associated the image with the forms and shapes picked up by my eyes and in the camera picture.

A sense of *knowing* filled me, a knowing that my dad had been there, greeting my mother and carrying her up … only, did that mean my dad was an angel? Was that possible? Not necessarily, I reasoned, messages from higher realms were often symbolic.

My dad was a wonderful man. Although I was adopted, he was the only father I knew, and he had a heart of gold! He had come over from Greece when he was 12 years old on the last boat that made it into the New York Harbor before World War I. He had worked as a bus boy and then a waiter in the restaurant business, learning English and saving and sending all the money he could back home as dowries for his seven sisters. One-by-one they were married off. It was only then, well in his thirties, that my dad considered marrying. My mother was from Louisiana, and had come up to the Washington, D.C. area with a girlfriend to work in the government. She was 19 years old when she married my dad. They loved to dance.

Dad went on to own several restaurants. This self-made man with a 7th grade education and the wisdom of the world learned through a vast array of experiences. He would help out pretty much anyone in need, and there were a series of people who moved through our lives as I was growing up, showing up when they needed some advice or a supporting hand. My mother, sister and I loved him and adored him, one of the few things the three of us had in common in an otherwise somewhat dysfunctional family relationship. Reflecting, it **was** possible. He might have been an angel.

Both happy and confused, I began to realize my whole world was turning upside down, or maybe more correctly I should say inside out. Not only was I talking to tiny spheres of electromagnetic energy, and interacting with forms and shapes made of plasma (?), but now I was asking questions and receiving answers, howbeit pictures that I had to interpret. Hmmm. Was there another way to ask questions?

David:

Was it plasma? While this was the closest word that seemed to make sense, it wasn't just right. In physics and chemistry plasma is a state of matter somewhat like gas in which a portion of the particles are ionized. Plasma is the most abundant form of matter in the Universe, the stuff of stars and inner-stellar space. It is a high energy electrically charged mix of ions and electrons that is electrically conductive such that it strongly responds to electromagnetic fields. Plasma appears on earth in places such as lightning bolts, flames, auroras and other fluorescent lights. However, natural plasma only exists at very high temperatures or in low temperature vacuums, where it is hard to maintain since it rapidly reacts to any molecules it encounters.

"Ectoplasm"—adding "ecto" (taken from the Greek "ektos" meaning outside) to "plasma"—was a term used in paranormal circles to describe the strange, mystical material that appeared to be manifested by mediums during a séance. In cell biology, ectoplasm is the outer part of the cytoplasm.

After a lengthy discussion, Alex and I were uncomfortable with calling the stuff Alex was capturing in her pictures "plasma." The only word that seemed to ring right to both of us was "*Myst*", purposefully spelled with a "y" to denote the magical, mystical and mysterious nature of the phenomenon. Having a word to describe this experience made conversation about it significantly easier, and we decided when we wrote about it in the future, we would italicize the word to emphasize the spelling.

One night—several weeks into this phenomenal experience—Alex began to catch the *Myst* in every picture, a wonderful stream of beautiful forms and shapes.

Alex began to catch a wonderful stream of beautiful forms and shapes.

While in this continuous stream of responses, she worked out a system to ask "yes/no" questions. She asked the *Myst* (or the intelligence behind the forming of the *Myst*) to come directly in front of her camera if the answer to a question she asked was YES; and to move away and not appear in her camera if the answer was NO. She would repeat this process three times for each question to ensure that the response she was getting was non-random. Further, following three answers that were the same (in the picture for YES, not in the picture for NO), Alex would validate the answer by asking the *Myst* to do the opposite of the answer, that is, if the answer to the question was YES (*Myst* in the picture), she would ask the *Myst* to GO AWAY for her next shot (number 4), and then COME BACK into her picture on shot number 5. Thus, **it took five pictures to ensure that each answer was correct and validated as a non-random pattern**.

While this process was cumbersome, it brought some degree of rigor into the asking. However, there were several drawbacks with this process. The greatest difficulty was remembering the questions to ask. It was difficult for Alex to remember questions when she was in such a state of joy interacting with the *Myst* and during those wonderful experiences the questions (and answers) just didn't seem all that important! Further, Alex was pondering what questions were appropriate to ask and not appropriate to ask? There was a learning curve in this regard.

An early series of questions included: *Are you electromagnetic energy?* The answer was YES. This was followed up with: *Is the electromagnetic energy of orbs part of the earth's ecosystem?* The answer was YES. Curious about their earlier discussion regarding plasma, Alex asked: *Can I use the term 'plasma' to describe you?* There was no hesitation, and the answer was YES. Then she asked if the word "*Myst*" was a good descriptive term and the answer was also YES. There was something quite endearing about these responses in terms of the intelligent source behind the phenomenon giving Alex and David options and choices.

Here are some of the questions that Alex asked, with the answers in parentheses after the question:

Does weather affect your ability to appear? (YES)

Will I be able to communicate with you in other ways? (YES)

Will I be able to use my computer to interact with you? (YES)

Can you go anywhere in the world? (YES)

Instantaneously? (YES)

Can you appear large and small? (YES)

Were some of the energies at TMI the same as the ones at MQI? (YES)

Can you go to other planets and star systems? (YES)

Is there more than one Universe? (YES)

Is there an Earth energy grid? (YES)

Before I came to the Earth system, am I from another star system? (YES)

Am I from Pliades? (NO) [This was the only system Alex could immediately recall.]

Do we have visitors from other planets here on Earth? (YES)

Will they make themselves generally known soon? (YES)

Will I get to meet them? (YES)

Have any of you been with me since I was born? (YES)

Have all of you been with me since I was born? (NO)

When I leave the Earth system will I be a spirit guide? (YES)

Is reincarnation real? (YES)

Alex quickly learned that there were some questions which would not be answered. She would regularly ask if her father, mother and sister were with her now. The answers were most often yes. The evening of October 24 she received a NO answer regarding her sister. Excited, she quickly asked, *Has she reincarnated?* On the first shot the answer was YES; on the next the answer was NO; and then the *Myst* disappeared for five shots. In other words, as described later by Alex to David, "It was none of my business!" After receiving this response Alex brought the *Myst* back in and carefully asked, *Has my sister started a new learning journey?* The answer was YES. To Alex it was clear, however, this learning journey was not another incarnation. The following evening Alex caught a picture of her sister riding a cloud just outside the front door. The next evening, Alex asked the *Myst*, *I had a feeling that the person on the cloud I captured yesterday in the camera was my sister Barbara. Was that her?* The answer was YES.

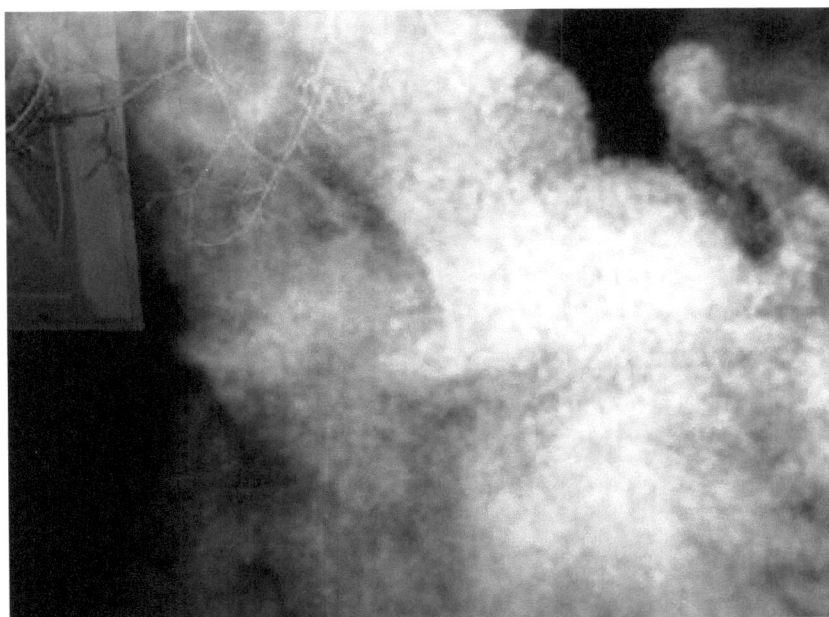

Right outside the front door Alex saw her sister riding a Myst cloud.

This was not the only type of question that received a YES, NO, and AWAY FOR 5 SHOTS response, although each time this sequence had different significance to Alex. One night she asked of the *Myst*, *Is a shift in consciousness under way?* and received a YES. However, when she strove to get more detail, each question was answered by the YES, NO, and AWAY FOR 5 SHOTS sequence. Then the thought floated through Alex's head, *This is not yet decided. It is up to You.* Alex knew that *You* was a plural representing the human race. ***Our future is up to us.***

Another time Alex was asking more personal questions. She asked, *Are you here to help me learn and grow?* and the answer was YES. She then asked, *Are you here to help David learn and grow?* and the answer was YES. Evidently, she and David were jointly tied to this growth experience. So, she asked, *Can I bring David out to see you?* and the answer was YES. Excited to know that this phenomenon was for others as well, Alex asked: *Am I supposed to share this?* A NO, YES and AWAY FOR 5 SHOTS sequence occurred. This was not a question they would answer, whoever they exactly was. As Alex interpreted, the decision was hers to make and was part of her learning experience. However, by inverting the order of the YES, NO response to NO, YES, the *Myst* was also suggesting that she consider it carefully. Both she and David would do so.

Alex:

The whole experience of figuring out a way to communicate in different ways was exciting! I was already getting "pictures" in response to some of my personal questions, and slowly learning to see the patterns in the pictures more clearly. Now I had a way to externally validate what was appearing in my external world, an approach that was not totally dependent on my own perception or translation of pictures. While admittedly this process still involved "me", it offered a first step towards greater understanding.

Having thought a great deal about the picture of my winged father carrying my mother up after her death, one question I asked was: Can human beings could become angels? The answer was YES. Remembering the response to my intimate question about my sister's possible reincarnation, I decided to stay away from my immediate family and ask about someone who I know would be an angel (given people COULD become angels).

In 1984 I had the wonderful opportunity to spend the good part of a day with Mother Teresa, privately interviewing her (with a translator … she spoke mostly French) and photographing her. [See Appendix B for a transcript of the article published following that visit.] This special day with Mother was the culmination of a life dream.

When I was in my early 30's and singing opera in Santa Barbara, California, at a Music Academy of the West event, I had several "old ladies" [probably my age now!] come up and ask for my autograph. "Of course," I smiled, grabbing their pen and the program. Then I froze. I couldn't remember my name! This "wake-up" call caused me to look carefully at myself. If I didn't really know who I was, then I needed to create who I was, the authentic me. So, I took the people who I admired the most (my father, Mother Teresa, and my mentor and voice coach Dr. Norman Sŏreng Wright) and explored the characteristics that had captured my admiration. While I could not be them, I could embed characteristics that I admired about them into my own being, and figure out the actions that would emerge out of those combined characteristics. How amazing to spend time with Mother Teresa less than 10 years later!

I knew that if any human being was to be an angel, it was Mother! So, I came out and asked the *Myst*, *Is Mother Teresa an angel?* A bright form appeared right in front of my flash. It was an angel. It was Mother. I captured a good part of her in the camera. While she was incredibly bright, like the full moon, with wonderful pinks accenting that brightness, I could perceive a loving face with long hair. In that "flash" of a second, love and joy permeated every part of my body.

For six weeks I continued questioning every night, that is, the nights I could REMEMBER the questions. David would help me prepare questions and I would review them before going out. Still, I often forgot them in the glory and light of my moments with the *Myst*.

(Above) A photograph of Mother Teresa taken by Alex in 1982 in Japan. (Below) The picture taken by Alex in 2010 when she asked if Mother Teresa was an angel. While Alex could see her face clearly, the light was so bright that Alex was thrilled to have the camera actually capture the moment.

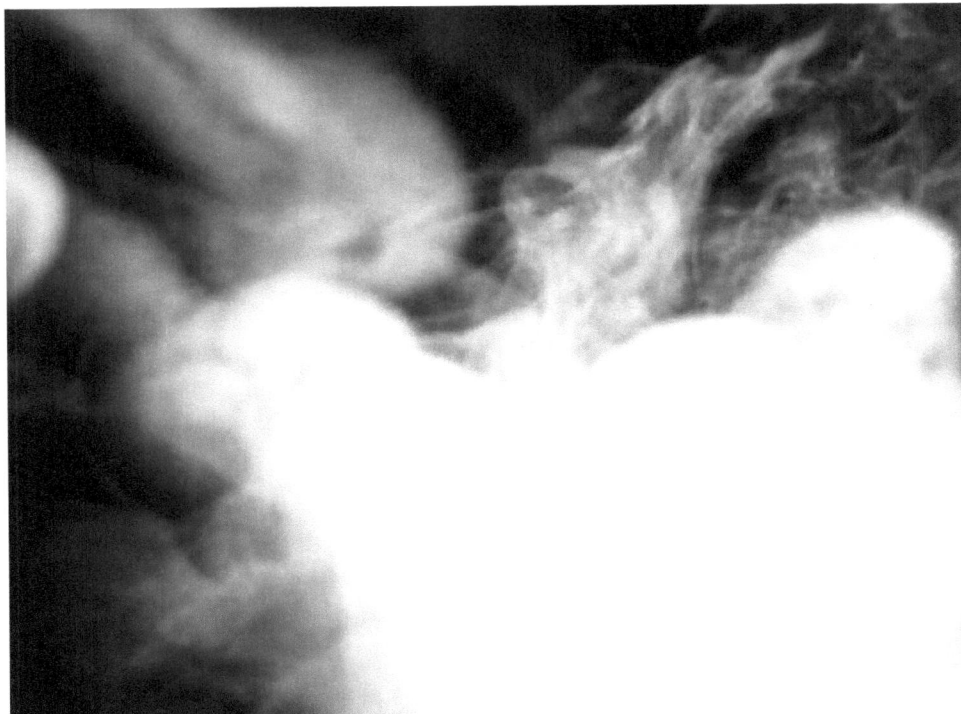

Chapter 6: Exploring the Myst

When Alex was in the midst of the *Myst*, she was in the NOW experience, and nothing else came into her mind, just a feeling of joy and love. When she was inside looking at the pictures, exploring the patterns, trying to perceive meaning she was filled with questions … and doubts. It was in this mode that she and David began to figure out how to move toward deeper understanding.

Since the Mountain Quest Inn and Retreat Center had a need for a new camera, Alex picked up a different brand of digital camera and tried that out one night. The light seemed to splash a bit more sideways, making it more difficult for her to see clearly what was happening in front of her, but still, she did see the *Myst*, and she did get pictures. That night when she came inside, Ginny and Jerry, Alex's daughter and son-in-law were visiting. David pulled up a number of *Myst* pictures on the overhead projector and the four of them sat and looked as the pictures came and went on the screen.

"Has anyone else gotten these pictures here?" asked Jerry.

"Not yet," responded Alex, "although David is planning on going out and trying." She then proceeded to tell Ginny and Jerry about her process of asking YES and NO questions, and shared some of the answers.

"If you two are game, let's try a little experiment," David suggested. Alex, Ginny and Jerry all agreed. "We will let Alex go out for about 10 minutes and see what she can get. Then each of us in turn will take 10 minutes, go to the very same spot using the same camera, and see what we can get." That seemed to make sense. Alex was first.

It was a beautiful night, a perfect early-winter setting, clear sky, temperature just below 40 degrees F, no wind. Alex went to the end of the garden where she had seen her first angel on October 6, and began singing softly, asking the *Myst* to form and shape for her tonight. Within a few minutes they were there, quite bright, and changing shapes and textures with each shot.

"Well?" Ginny, Jerry and David chimed in as Alex walked back through the double doors into the retreat center where they sat waiting. Alex pulled out the memory card from the camera and copied the pictures onto her computer hard drive. Since her computer was already hooked up to the overhead, it was only a moment before the pictures were projected on the screen. They were beautiful.

"Now tell us how you got these," Ginny asked, as Alex put the memory card back into her camera. So Alex went through the process she used.

"First, I always make sure any worries and my "to-do" list and even the noise that seems to often move through my head is gone. I send it all up to my higher Self, imagining flows of color moving through my head chakra and upward to the file cabinet my higher Self maintains for me (and regularly empties out as these thoughts become unneeded). When I am in the NOW—with just a pleasant feeling of being and floating—I take a deep breath of love, fill my body with that, and then breathe out a bubble of light and love around me. Then I start singing, calling on my beautiful angels of light, asking the *Myst* to shape and form for me tonight." And she sang a strain of the melody.

Jerry was the first one out. No *Myst*. David was the second one out. While he did not get any *Myst* pictures that night, he would soon. Finally, it was Ginny's turn.

Now Ginny has a beautiful singing voice, and telephone callers repeatedly have difficulty telling the difference between Ginny's voice and Alex's voice. Perhaps [or perhaps not] this has something to do with why Ginny captured a wisp of *Myst* in one picture. Whatever the reason, it was there.

The next evening, after asking permission, Alex took David out with her to photograph the *Myst*. While in the beginning his focus was on seeing it, by the third experience David was able to capture the *Myst* a few times with his own camera, and by the fourth he was a bit more fluid in his capture, and was on his own, that is, taking photographs from another spot on the farm.

David's first experience playing with the Myst.

David:

You cannot see the *Myst* until the camera flash occurs. Just before the flash there is a red light sensor flash. I recall that first night was quite dark. With practice I learned to watch directly in front of the camera so that I could see the *Myst* when the camera flashed. It worked. However, the flash was so fast (about a millisecond) that my eyes could not follow the pattern of the *Myst*—but by looking in the back of the camera after the picture was taken the pattern could be clearly seen. It was very exciting to experience taking pictures at night that often yielded nonrandom patterns of *Myst*, that is, a low concentration of water molecules.

I found that sometimes I could get them and sometimes not. On the other hand, I have a terrible singing voice so I didn't attempt to "call them in" as Alex did so often. Rather, I just mentally invited them into my picture. I also wanted to check out the possibility of these patterns coming from my breath. Sure enough, I found that if I blew my breath in front of the camera while taking the picture the picture would show the outline of the breath. So I then started holding my breath or turning my face away from the front of the camera. I still got patterns of the *Myst* in the camera shots. So that helped confirm the *Myst* was not a picture of our breath.

What was so amazing to me is that there was a whole new world outside our front door just waiting to be uncovered, perhaps understood, and enjoyed. However, I still wondered, what do the patterns represent? Why are they here? Who are they? What information and especially what knowledge can they bring to us? And, what are "they" composed of? Or is "they" even the proper word to use?

At the end of October Alex was scheduled to attend her second *Starlines II* at TMI. While Alex truly enjoys basking in the higher energies, all of the daily deep dives into the realms of the inner world were underpinned with her nightly visits to the large rose crystal that sat at the top of the mountain, not far from the TMI facility. She would wait until the group that gathered in the parlor dwindled to a few people, then would quietly take her leave and walk the short distance to the crystal. She would sit on the concrete stool beside the crystal and move through her meditation, then walk a few feet toward the tree line and call in the *Myst*.

That first night, and the next four nights, it only took a few minutes before Alex's visitors appeared. As she returned to the parlor that first night, some late-night conversations were still underway. Alex sat at the table and pulled the pictures up on her computer for the small group to see. They were elated, and excited! One young man pushed her, "Do you think I can see them?"

"I don't know," responded Alex.

"Will you go out with me?" he asked. So she did, right then and there. But no matter what he did, the young man was not able to see the *Myst*, and it did not appear to Alex while he was present. Finally, he went in to bed. Alex stayed outside for a few minutes longer, and yes, the *Myst* was there for her again and again.

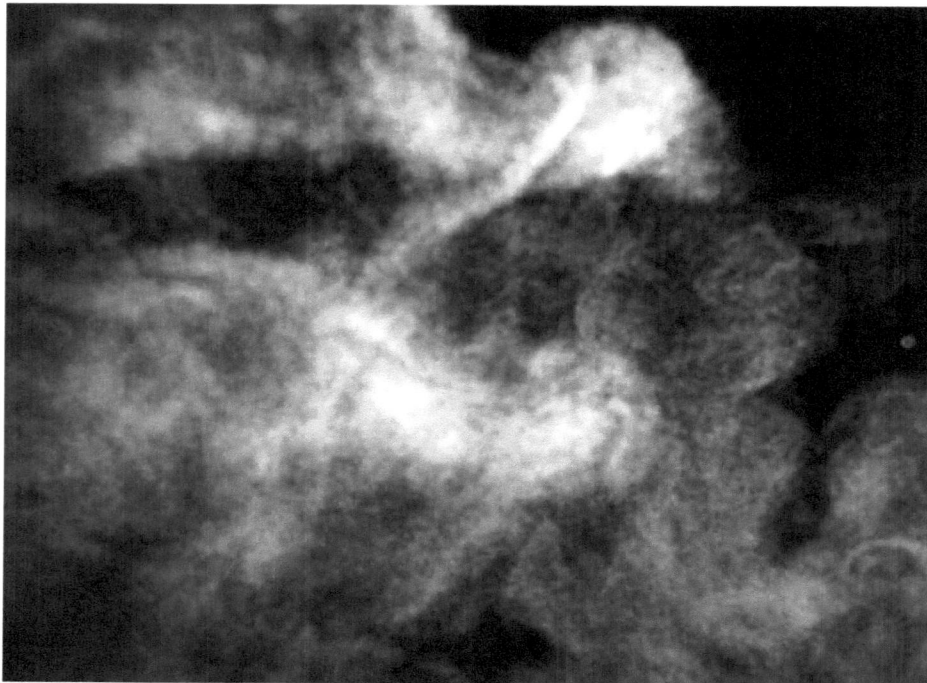

The Myst pictures taken at TMI were unique,
and just as beautiful as the ones taken at Mountain Quest.

The second day at TMI a small group went out with her to see if they could catch the *Myst*. They were not successful; but after they left, Alex again had a delightful interaction with the *Myst*. Alex began to wonder how an individual's energy affected the experience. That seemed to make sense given the earlier non-response when she had gone outside with the mental focus of "just" taking pictures.

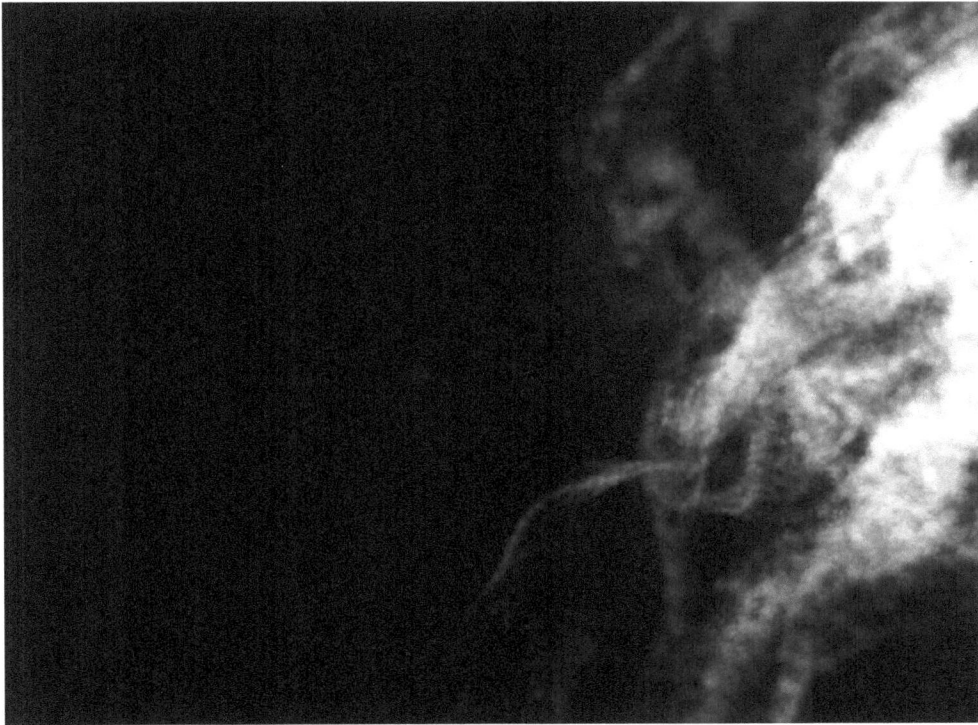

*This unusual picture of what has been described by others as an elf
has been shared with members of the TMI Professional Group.*

The third evening one of the workshop leaders, a psychologist who had been in the small group of late conversationalists the first night, asked if she could see the newest pictures. She was amazed with them. "I've been thinking about this," she told Alex. "And asking why you?" That question had been on Alex's mind since the beginning of the phenomenon. Alex responded with that thought.

The psychologist smiled up at Alex from where she sat in front of the computer. "I think it just makes good sense," she continued. "You have solid educational credentials, are the former Chief Knowledge Officer of the U.S. Department of the Navy, and have authored several books. Simultaneously, you are on your journey toward spiritual awakening, open to new ideas, and are a researcher married to a scientist. And, from the looks of all these pictures, you seem to have an incredible quality of persistence. To begin with, I would never have had the patience to catalog over 10,000 orbs! Perhaps you are the perfect person to have the experience of the *Myst*."

This week event at TMI provided Alex and David both additional perspectives and one more piece of knowledge to the puzzle of the *Myst*. Yes, Alex could get the *Myst* pictures in other locations. The Bennets now had pictures from a a second location to compare to the pictures from the Mountain Quest Institute complex in their continuing quest to learn more about the behaviors of the *Myst*.

Chapter 7: The Parting of the Fog

The fall moved quickly into winter, a cold winter, but Alex didn't notice. She layered up and spent hours each night out with the *Msyt*. She warmed herself in between photo shoots by climbing into bed next to David, who always generated a high level of heat. Then, when the sun was up, she would sit in front of the computer to look through the night's pictures. She pushed through each day exhausted, still, able to do the work that needed to be done. Not that there wasn't a toll to pay for her lack of sleep. The bedroom was splayed with clothes, the bathroom had powder building up on the floor, and her office, well, it looked like her office. Alex had the unique ability to focus on the work at hand and not notice the mess around her. On the other hand, David noticed it. Yet he kept quiet, and still showed an interest in the special pictures Alex exclaimed about each morning.

One afternoon, a colleague was visiting with her small son. Kumo, the beautiful 120-pound male Akita, was his usual self, soft and loving. Out of habit, Alex bent over with her hands on her knees and excitedly made noises at him. This was a daily game between Kumo and David and Alex. Kumo always squenched down, wagged his tail and chipped off short barks which almost sounded like laughter. Then they would hug.

This morning was different. When Kumo squenched down the short barks morphed into something large, pulling a deep growl from within, deafening and frightening. Alex jumped back with Kumo as the nearby child started to cry. Kumo didn't seem to be able to pull himself out of the growling state; it took several minutes of soothing words from Alex before he stood up and, exhausted, curled up on the floor. Later that evening Alex shared what had happened with David. They were both worried. Kumo's older sister Sashi had died earlier in the year at the age of 14. Kumo was now 10.

The next morning when he rose, David went over to Kumo and leaned next to him for the ritual morning neck rub. Instantly, Kumo's head flipped up and the deep growl bubbled up turning into a ferocious sound which did not stop quickly. Now it was David who quickly pulled back, just out of reach as Kumo's teeth snapped together.

Alex was on the phone as soon as the vet's office opened. Their regular vet was off, but a partner on duty took the call. Together, they went through the symptoms and events. Unfortunately, there were several other pieces of the pie that quickly came up … Kumo had been dripping a bit at the mouth, a foamy dripping, which was unusual, and several days earlier he had killed a skunk out in front of the house. While he was up-to-date on his rabies shots, the vet was very concerned, talking about responsibility and other such things. David and Alex were frightened for Kumo. This was their beloved dog; the two Akitas were their children.

It was with heavy heart that they called Andrew, Alex's youngest son who now managed the Inn and Retreat Center, and who had helped raise the dogs, to address this serious issue. Kumo lay in the next room sleeping. They acted quickly. Because of the Retreat Center, there were people continuously in and out of the house; Alex and David did not have their own house, but slept and worked in rooms on the second floor of the 110-year-old farm house. A 120-pound animal out of control could not be allowed on the premises. After talking to the veterinarian and looking at the details of Kumo's recent behavior, the only solution was to put Kumo down. As it turned out when the state veterinarian did the autopsy, Kumo didn't have rabies; rather, there was some neurological damage in his brain.

Alex was incredibly distraught. She really felt a need to see the *Myst*, but it was windy over the weekend. The *Myst* didn't appear when it was windy. Then Monday night when she opened the front door to go out there was thick fog across the valley. The next day Alex and David would be going up to Washington, D.C. to speak at a conference, and they wouldn't be back until the following weekend. Standing at the door looking out, Alex couldn't imagine waiting until then, but how could the *Myst* form and shape in the fog? You wouldn't be able to tell the difference!

She reflected for just a moment, and then her heart won over her head. She grabbed the camera and headed out, circling to the left to the back parking lot. The fog was continuous; she couldn't see more than 10-15 feet around her. Still, she needed/wanted to see the *Myst*. She began singing softly, then increased her tone, explaining in song the situation and sending her love, asking the *Myst* to come. The first few pictures were lots of fog circles punctuated with a few orbs, whose light and internal configuration gave them a distinct look. She kept singing.

It happened quickly, across maybe five camera shots. The fog thinned, then cleared for about 20 feet around Alex, and the *Myst* formed and shaped right in front of her camera. She couldn't believe it, but kept singing, weeping in happiness. She stayed in the clearing for another ten minutes, reveling in the beauty of the *Myst* and feeling the love and joy that accompanied their visits.

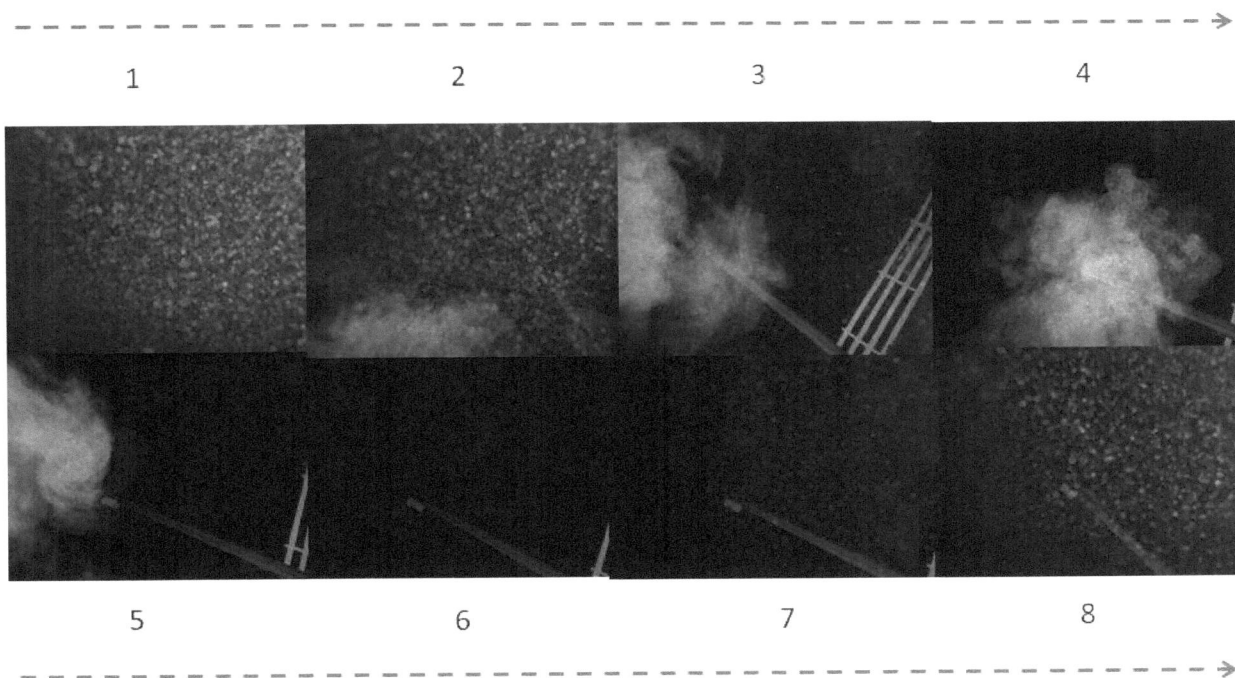

While these photographs are in sequence, there are a number of photographs in between that have been removed. For example, there are half a dozen fog pictures before the Myst appears, and several dozen photographs of the Myst once the fog cleared.

Then it was over. The *Myst* was gone and the fog quickly closed around her. And now Alex could sleep.

The next weekend she was out again. Both the night and *Myst* were beautiful. The pictures were some of her best, and since the *Myst* was coming in a continuous stream, she began to ask questions, and had excellent response.

Then, in song, Alex prayed to her angels and guides to please take care of their previous Kumo, to watch over him. A circle of *Myst* appeared very small and bright right in front of the camera lens. A few shots later there was larger *Myst* that was shaped like a dog. Kumo? Her heart beating, an expectation was building within Alex, and a joy was building in the sadness that had attached itself to her since Kumo's loss.

The expectation was well grounded. The picture that had been formed in the round circle stood out immediately. It was the answer to her plea. What must be her was pictured at the bottom right, hands clasped in prayer. Right in front of her being pulled up a *Myst*y slope was the form of a large dog. A kneeling angel was reaching down to the collar, and another with open wings was watching above. Right behind the kneeling angel was a figure which looked like it represented Mother Mary, and behind her was a large angel with pink swirls throughout. Alex's inner voice informed, "The angel of compassion." Alex didn't know his name, but was incredibly thankful to them all.

Alex calls this photograph "The Journey Home."

Alex:

I really miss our beloved dogs … they were our family. I learned so much from them. From Sashi, loyalty; from Kumo, gentleness and peace; and from both, unconditional love. It's hard to explain, but when I saw the pictures I felt, simultaneously, tears of love and joy, and sadness. It was an extraordinary night! Several shots after "The Journey Home" there was a clear picture of Kumo, and behind him, a dark shadow that I'm sure is Sashi! You can see Kumo's proud stand, Akita all the way, with his lovely tail proudly curled. His back legs, well, they look more like wings, just like I told him they were meant to be. When he was young, our beautiful Kumo had been through four surgeries for hip dysplasia. His back legs were always weak. Now, they WERE wings! I always told him they were meant to be wings.

*And right behind the beautiful winged Akita that was Kumo was
the dark head of Alex's beloved Sashi, who had passed the previous winter.*

This night somehow changed things. I always knew—in the sense of a knowing—about death, that is, only being a transition. But there was our beloved Kumo right in front of me in the light! Again, my insides were banging up against my outsides. And in the banging, I was filled with so much appreciation and love.

David:

We were pretty sure that whatever intelligence was creating the *Myst* was using the materials at hand, specifically, the water in the air. When Alex told me the story of the fog and showed me the photographs, this helped confirm that assumption. I began to explore the materiel aspects of water. Is it possible for mist to take specific shapes? My own belief is yes.

Water can have its properties and hence its structure changed in nonlinear ways without any change of composition, with structure defined as a specific three-dimensional arrangement of atoms and molecules. Notice that water structure is different from its composition, which is made up of hydrogen and oxygen atoms combining to form water molecules. Research at Penn State University and other universities has supported this thesis that water can have many different structures. One researcher noted that there may be as many as 64 possible changes of water from one form to another!

Water has many different and striking properties and seems to be able to form clusters of molecules of different shapes and sizes. These clusters may be sensitive to electromagnetic fields. To me this implies the possibility and feasibility that the *Myst*, composed of water droplets, could be influenced by electric and magnetic fields in a manner that could create the shapes and patterns shown in the *Myst*-Art pictures that Alex, myself and some others have taken. At this point in the research I offer this as a reasonable exposition, but to my knowledge it has not been researched sufficiently to be sure.

While the above discussion does not prove that the pictures are created by some "external force," it does imply the possibility. I do believe the shapes and patterns in the pictures are not random. That conclusion is discussed further in volume II of the *Myst* series, *Patterns in the Myst*.

Chapter 8: Women of Wisdom

By the time the Women of Wisdom held their Fall retreat at the Mountain Quest Retreat Center, Alex had taken over 30,000 photographs. She and David had decided to offer the pictures as "art" so that people could make up their own opinions about them. At first, Alex had wanted to just flood the Internet with them, sharing with everyone. But David quickly convinced her that with no context, viewers would just think she was taking pictures of smoke or breath or water or dust. No, he said, this phenomenon required some context, and further study.

So, Alex and David spent a great deal of their time running small experiments, and studying the patterns in the *Myst*, which no doubt will be the subject of the next volume in this series.

Alex had finally come to a place of balance. She no longer needed to go out three times a night; and she no longer worried that the *Myst* wouldn't return. She KNEW they would be there when the weather conditions were right, and if she was in resonance with them.

Several friends and visitors at the Inn had been able to see the *Myst* over Alex's shoulder, and a few had captured their own pictures. Others had tried and failed, sometimes on the same night in the same place where another would get a picture. A long-time friend and colleague, who dates back to Alex's work as Co-Chair of the Federal Knowledge Management Working Group and has been a regular visitor to Mountain Quest, became incredibly excited when Alex shared a picture of the *Myst*.

A Letter from Susan:

Dear Alex and David --

I write to you about *Myst*-Art from my heart and my own experience. As you know, I have been at the Mountain Quest Inn over the years and have mentioned to you that I have seen or felt mystical beings in the valley and hills surrounding your property. Alex, I also remember sharing with you that I constantly saw a small but friendly "protector" on your left shoulder. This being may have been described as a fairy or guardian, but I felt the being filled with love and protection. Anyway, I did not know at that time that in short order I would have a grand mal seizure or two, which have enabled me further entrée to what is perhaps a world of beings that can only be seen and felt in an electromagnetic world. Perhaps these visions are a fraction of the information that our brains filter out … and my brain stopped filtering. I shared this with you.

Somehow, it seems that concurrent with my neurological and own spiritual shifting, you and David were exploring the *Myst* with digital photography, pixels, flash, love, joy and intent. While through different paths, I am thinking that we—and others—are drawing in these energies, these protectors/guardians. Assuredly we are not alone. Anyway, I had no idea you were doing this until one day I received a photo that you shared with me. I almost fainted, for there in front of me was a multi-dimensional photo of the realm that I can see in my day-to-day life! I was completely astonished.

I was breathing most heavily and very excitedly when I called you and asked how you did this, what on earth was going on that you figured this out, and said **THANK YOU**! You explained the really easy process to me and I could not wait to come to Mountain Quest again to try this out. In early spring I had that opportunity and it was great. Although this first time I did not get photos of angels and spirits similar to those on your website, I did get orbs and some amazing and unusual cloud shots. One photo clearly showed what looked to me like an angel hovering over Mountain Quest. Since I am highly photosensitive, this was also a challenge to me as I was not only taking photos in the dark, I was taking photos with my eyes closed!

You and David explained to me that I should not be disappointed. Alex, you spent three months singing to orbs before the *Myst* appeared! And then, it was Fall. You told me that the *Myst* appeared more easily in the cooler weather and the photos of the angels and other images that you were most successful in obtaining were mainly accomplished during the winter season. (I have been counting the days since Spring by the way.)

The real progress for me took hold when I got home and began to go out at night and pray and sing in my back yard. The first photo I got was a photo that looked like hands over my house in a pose of energetic protection—very much like Reiki (I am a Reiki Master). Another photo, taken during the day, shows energy rising up right in front of me while I was taking photos of trumpet flowers. I didn't see this energy when I was taking the photo. I have also gotten photos of strange beings in one of my trees, orb showers, incredible clouds, images in my bushes that look very much like angels, and many, many faces in the orbs. I still can hardly wait until winter though!

Through all of this, I maintain a deep gratitude toward you for sharing this amazing gift for anyone who wants to learn more about the *Myst*. More than that, you are inviting in loving energies and making connections which may someday not only increase our knowledge of our own world, but many worlds of which we can only dream.

The Women of Wisdom Group

The Women of Wisdom is a group of "wise and wonderful women honoring and celebrating the divine." The mindfulness attributes they strive to practice throughout the retreat experience (and their lives) are listening, patience, trust, allowance, awareness and being present. While the retreat is gently structured with yoga, sharing sessions, meditations, singing and dancing sessions, healing sessions, a Shamanic Ritual, gift giving, a talent show, and bonfires, it is also an experience in the NOW, co-evolving with the wishes/desires/needs of the participants. For four days in October 2011, a group of 34 Women of Wisdom filled the Mountain Quest facilities.

The Women of Wisdom dance with the orbs in the Great Room of the Mountain Quest Retreat Center.

The energy of their interactions was spectacular. On a more pragmatic level, Alex had never seen this number of women live in close quarters for a period of four days without a single conflict arising! Further, they were continuously in service to each other, freely sharing their thoughts, beliefs and skills while staying open and respectful of other's thoughts, beliefs and skills. Little wonder that the *Myst* was strong during this time period, and that so many of these women were able to either take photographs of, or be photographed with, the *Myst*.

From Margie:

While visiting the Inn at Mountain Quest with the WOW (Women of Wisdom) retreat for women, my roommate and I went out two mornings to see if we could photograph some orb pictures. We are both Reiki Masters and body workers, so we hoped we could do this on our own without Alex as we did not want to bother her at 6 am in the morning. It was cold out, probably in the high 30's with the mist hanging low. We hugged each other as we walked and sang songs such as *Amazing Grace*. We were surprised to see that our photographs were filled with round circular orbs even though we only had a 5.1 pixel camera. We took pictures by the barn, in the trees and in the labyrinth. The labyrinth pictures were the most intense. We actually got the orbs to begin shaping, mostly into faces. I kept asking the orbs to shape into a heart and, finally, one of the pictures did present with a heart. Alex was very impressed at what we were able to capture on our first two times out.

The first evening of my stay in the Scholars Room, I dreamed an orb entered my body while I was sleeping. I felt so peaceful when this happened. During the four days I was at Mountain Quest, off and on I would get images of white light shapes around the trees and people and above groups. I am able to see this usually anywhere I am; however, at Mountain Quest it was always more intense and larger!

On the second evening we went out with Alex and she showed us some of the techniques she uses. When you see the *Myst* right in front of the camera flash (using the red sensor light), then you know you will have a picture of the orbs/*Myst*. Other than swirling in the red sensor light, note you do not "see" anything in the air until the flash goes off. Alex gave me one of her extra cameras to use. I went down the dirt road by the white fence containing the Llamas.

I decided rather than singing, I would ground and center and feel blissful peace in my heart. I was able to photograph two amazing images: one that looks like a dog head (DSC06566) and the other like a lightning bolt that then turned into an animal jumping over the fence (DSC06569).

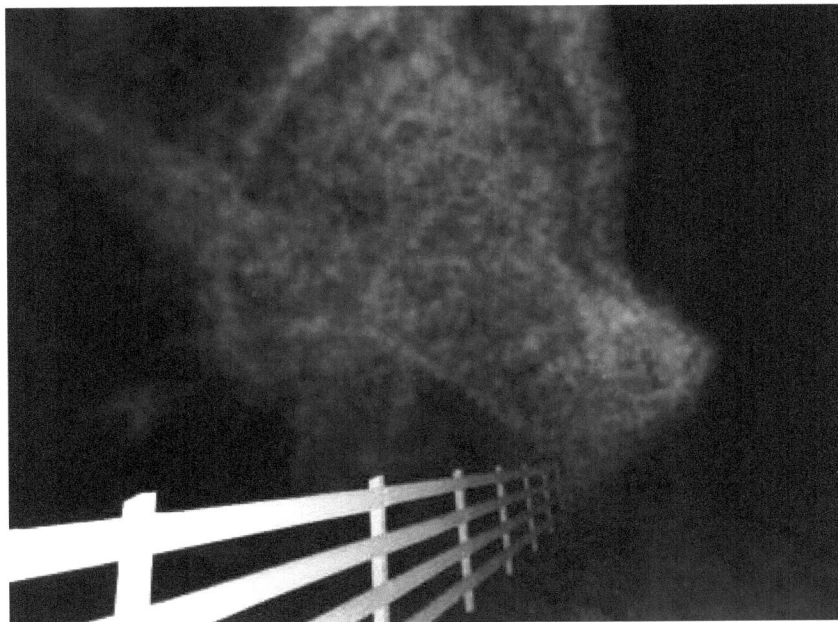

One looks like a dog's head and the other (top of next page) like a lightning bolt
that then turned into an animal jumping over the fence.

My oldest son passed away from complications of leukemia and diabetes nine years ago, so I had hoped to get an image of Keith. So, I was requesting this in my intention prior to going out to film. I think the strong emotion of love I felt for Keith may have helped me get the two images that I did capture.

From Tamara:

The Women of Wisdom (WOW) fourth annual retreat at Mountain Quest Institute was especially memorable. After an opening ceremony filled with singing and joy, Alex led four of us at 11 pm in a process to see and photograph orbs.

My experience of orbing resulted in a life-changing "aha" moment for me. Through vibration, vocalizing, harmonics, and singing, I realized I could see, hear, feel and intuit more of the expressions of life all around me. As my dear mentor would say, "Life is full of life." While I already knew that feeling is important to prayer in action, my orbing experience transformed my thoughts and understanding into a deeply felt personal truth. For a long time, singing has brought me joy and a perceptible feeling of being connected to all. It is a revelation that through harmonics, this orbing experience has been so extraordinary for me that I want to re-tell it to others.

When first starting the orb experience, it occurred to me it was in my head because I did not know the words or the tune I was singing. And as a result, I noticed I was not feeling completely and powerfully connected to divine life force. As I observed my thoughts, I felt the anxiety of not being able to see anything. Then, as I gently returned my attention to singing and feeling in the moment, I did see sparkles and cloud *Myst* orb formations.

Alex suggested each of us in the group try orbing by ourselves while she photographed each of us from a distance. When I was alone and playing with the orbing process, I sang harmony-filled songs I know well (ones I sing during walks and in a musical trio). I opened my heart. In this immense expansive connected state, I saw orb sparkles and orb cloud patterns as the camera flashed in my close field of vision. It makes me laugh now to have had reports the next morning from two friends in separate rooms, "We heard your voice singing last night."

When I was orbing by myself, Alex took a picture of me with a distinctive large *Myst* extending from my left arm. I remember feeling soaring reverence and glory and the divine presence of life force while singing and deeply praying to see more of life. During this really loud singing, I was seeking intently to see the face of my spiritual mentor, who transitioned at age 99 in 2009. It does not surprise me that my deep caring for my dear mentor, Polly Thomas, could possibly be captured in a photograph in this orbing experience.

Tamara interacting with the Myst.

I know what this experience means to me; I am sharing it as my truth not "the truth." In disclosing my orbing experience, it is my intent to add to the chorus that "life is full of life" and expansive feelings combined with vocalizing and harmonics can lead to experiencing more of life all around us. It is delightful to continue pondering and feeling what this orbing experience gave me about how life works.

From Liz:

While attending a retreat at Mountain Quest Inn, I went out with a harpist and we sang and invited the orbs to come to us so we could see them. That night I was disappointed that I didn't see them, or get a picture of any mist orbs. But the next night, after bringing Reiki (Divine energy) to other retreat members most of the afternoon, I was overflowing with energy. We all came together to sing around the bonfire, and I was blessed by the *Myst* over me.

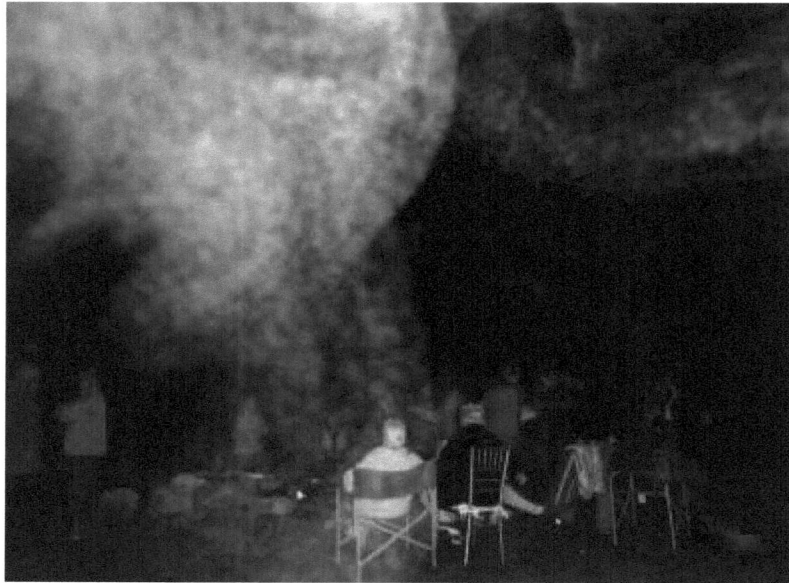

The Myst connects with Liz as the WOW group talks and sings around the campfire.

[In a follow-on email:] I feel so blessed and engaged with the energy … am most appreciative that you [Alex] caught that [in the picture]. You will always be a part of my memories of that mystical place where you and David reside and where you are in my heart, mind and soul.

From Kathy:

Upon arriving at Mountain Quest, the view of the hills and the trees with the Inn nestled within a valley is breathtaking.

On Friday evening we opened our gathering [Women of Wisdom] with drumming that helped to bring everyone together as one for the wonderful weekend that was about to unfold. After the drumming and singing was complete, I was introduced to a Hemi-Sync® Meditation, *The Visit*. I was able to follow the guidance fairly well, and my experience [on this inner journey] was that as I was leaving the cave I saw a space ship and what looked like a being going back into the ship. I did not have any conversation, but was told that I will remember more. I did see a silhouette of my parents as I entered the cave, but again no dialog and the image faded.

Afterwards, we went outside to play with the *Myst* and orbs! What a wonderful experience to be able to see the orbs in the flash of the camera's light. The orbs are so pretty and bright, like little sparks of diamonds because of the clarity of the sparks. And they love to play! I love the picture of Tamara [another WOW retreat participant] with the orbs! In one of the pictures that was taken it looks like orbs are shooting directly into my head. It resembles what a comet looks like but not as dense.

What fun!

Friday was a very busy high energy day with an opening ceremony in the labyrinth followed by very powerful chanting and shamanic journeying. In my journey, I put myself in a bubble and floated up into the clouds and there I met a little girl (me?) who was sitting in an oversized chair made of clouds. I was invited to sit. I climbed into the chair and we just floated around in a state of "just being". It was very comforting and relaxing …

*The Myst streaks down toward the singing WOW group
with a streak of light landing on Kathy's head.*

Saturday was amazing as well. Darlene and I got up early and took our drums and her flute and hiked up to the first hill to greet the day. The mist was amazing. As we were drumming we noticed that the mist was all around us, but not within our energy field. When Darlene switched to playing her flute, I noticed the mist receding into the low lands, but was able to the see mist swirling about as if it were dancing.

Darlene suggested that we sing to the mist and request it to take shape for us, so we started to sing something very simple. The mist started to come back up the hill, very dense, and surround us again! When we stopped singing it went back down into the valley. Then we noticed the aura of the land, which was a brilliant white glow! Up came the sun over the hill. WOW! We could see different colors and shades of purple and blue and pink in and around the sun. As we looked to the far right the sky was an indigo blue and as we looked to the left and behind us the sky was a very deep lavender color. That morning we were told that the horses ran, happily, out of the barn too!

From Kathy Several Weeks after Her Visit

Life after my wonderful experience at Mountain Quest Institute:

After leaving the WOW Re-treat held at Mountain Quest Inn, I am finding myself more open and aware of the life force that is in and all around us. I'm noticing the mists and greeting them with delight, and in turn the mist is showing me its wonderful, beautiful colors! I find myself marveling at the grass waving as wind flows across it, sensing that the grass is delighted, and I am playful with it. All of nature seems to be more alive and brilliant. The waters are singing and the trees are dancing and I am in awe of this magnificent symphony that is playing all around me all the time. All I have to do is watch and listen. And when I stop to listen and see, the beauty of the world reveals itself to me in the most beautiful, playful and loving way.

The orbs are amazing to say the least. Again, an experience that left me in awe! What beauty to see with the naked eye in the night in the flash of a camera. When we were outside in the night I felt a very playful and loving energy around us. It made me laugh out loud. I felt like a child playing with snowflakes that look like millions of tiny little diamonds floating around in the air. The energy is alive and very tangible at Mountain Quest.

Now I feel light and airy yet stronger in my truth. There is a quiet confidence in me that has been released since my visit to Mountain Quest. It has moved me closer to knowing the truth of who I am. I feel a loving presence within me that does not need to be defended or expressed, it just is. Some repetitive old thought patterns have been replaced with more positive thoughts of compassion and love. I am noticing a release of wanting to control outcomes and find myself more open to honoring and accepting other people on their journey. What a relief and a gift of letting go!

God is everywhere present, and since visiting Mountain Quest I feel much closer to this truth. Alex and Dave have created a safe, beautiful and magical place where you can go and allow yourself to open up to the universe and know that all is perfect and in Divine right order here and now!

Alex and David:

Our heads and hearts were spinning from the experiences that others were beginning to have. And there were so many questions emerging. Was Mountain Quest special? Certainly, we know that is true. It is a natural setting with wonderful energy, and there is always so much love here. By now we also knew that the phenomenon of the *Myst* was not an isolated event. There were other people in the past and the present having the same experiences in different places around the world. Although some of them were reluctant to share this widely, others were publishing books loaded with pictures, and sharing their personal insights on this wonderful experience. Take a look at Sandra Underwood's book *Orbs, Lightwaves, and Cosmic Consciousness*, Miceal Ledwith's inspiring work on the Internet, and Klaus and Gundi Heinemann's book *Orbs: Their Mission and Messages of Hope.*

Still, there is so much we've learned yet to share, and so much more to learn. **So, we continue this journey into the *Myst*, and invite you to take this journey with us. This book is just the beginning.**

Endnotes

1: We define knowledge as the capacity (potential or actual) to take effective action. See Bennet, A., Bennet, D. and Avedisian, J. (2018), *The Course of Knowledge,* Frost, WV: MQIPress.

2: The Monroe Institute (TMI) was founded in 1974 by Robert Monroe, a ground-breaking visionary and explorer of human consciousness. His pioneering research, beginning in the 1950s, led to the discovery that specific sound patterns have identifiable, beneficial effects on our capabilities. Tens of thousands of people have journeyed from around the world to attend TMI's life-enhancing on-campus programs. These programs, conducted at the Institute's training facilities in Virginia, are dedicated to developing, exploring, and applying expanded states of consciousness using the extraordinary Hemi-Sync® sound technologies. See www.monroeinstitute.org

3: Binaural beats were identified in 1839 by H.W. Dove, a German experimenter. In the human mind, binaural beats are detected with carrier tones (audio tones of slightly different frequencies, one to each ear) below approximately 1500 Hz. The mind perceives the frequency differences of the sound coming into each ear, mixing the two sounds to produce a fluctuating rhythm and thereby creating a beat or difference frequency. Because each side of the body sends signals to the opposite hemisphere of the brain, both hemispheres must work together to "hear" the difference frequency. This perceived rhythm originates in the brainstem and is neurologically routed to the reticular formation, then moves to the cortex where it can be measured as a frequency-following response. This inter-hemispheric communication is the setting for brain-wave coherence, which facilitates whole-brain cognition, that is, an integration of left- and right-brain functioning. See Bennet, A. and Bennet, D. (2020), "The Human Knowledge System: Music and Brain Coherence" in Bullard, B. and Bennet, A., *Remembrance: Pathways to Expanded Learning*, Frost, WV: MQIPress, pp 123-142.

4: The **Cognitive Capabilities** identified were *Noticing* (the ability to observe around us and recognize those things relevant to our immediate needs), *Scanning* (the ability to review and survey a large amount of data and information and selectively identify areas of relevance), *Patterning* (the ability to review, study and interpret large amounts of data/events/information and identify causal or correlative connections that over time or space may represent patterns driven by underlying phenomena which may be crucial to understanding the situation at hand), *Sensing* (the ability to take inputs from the external world through our five senses and ensure the translation of those inputs into our mind to represent as accurate a transduction process as possible), and *Integration* (the top-level capacity to take large amounts of data and information and pull it together to identify meaning or, as frequently called, sensemaking). The internal **Cognitive Processes** that support the Cognitive Capabilities were: *Visualizing* (the methodology of focusing attention on a given area and through imagination and logic create an internal vision and scenario for success); *Intuiting* (the art of making maximum use of our own intuition developed carefully through experience, trial and error, and deliberate internal questioning and application; includes the aspect of empathy, the ability to take oneself out of oneself and put oneself into another person's world); *Valuing* (the capability to observe situations and recognize the value underlying their various aspects, and the ability to align your vision, mission and goals to focus attention on the immediate situation at hand; includes full awareness of personal values and beliefs); and *Judging* (the ability to develop conclusions and interpretations through the use of rules of thumb, facts, knowledge and experiences, and intuition). See Bennet, A. and Bennet, D. (2020), "The Art of Knowing" in Bennet, A., Bennet, D., Shelley, A., Bullard, T., and Lewis, Jr., *The Profundity and Bifurcation of Change Part I: Laying the Groundwork*, Frost, WV: MQIPress, pp 153-171. Or, see Bennet, A. (2018), *Possibilities that are YOU! Volume 10: Knowing*, Frost, WV: MQIPress.

Appendix A: Alex's Meditation

This is the meditation that has emerged over the years. Alex moves through this every evening, dependent on her mindset and feelings sometimes rapidly and more rote, but most often pausing and listening throughout, bookmarking moments of pure being and bliss.

[Emptying]

I fill all my bodies with light . . .

… my physical body, my etheric body, my astral body, my mental body, my intuitive body, my spiritual body and any other bodies that are mine. And into this light from all of my bodies I pull every bit of negativity, any negative thought, feeling and emotion, and anything else that will bring about negativity.

And into this light from all of my bodies I pull anything that in any way will slow, hamper or prevent my doing the following: achieving my life's goals, achieving the greater good, achieving the full potential of all of my bodies, learning and growing continuously. Being all I can be, doing all I can do, and being the best person I can be in terms of the greater good. Being connected to all that is and filled with love, joy, happiness, peace, health, strength, courage and wisdom, and using all of this to create more of God's thought.

And I pull into the light anything that in any way will bring about harm, illness, pain or degeneration to any of my bodies, and any dark matter, dark energy and any fear, and anything that in any way will bring about or support fear.

And I pull into the light anything that in any way will slow, hamper or prevent using this body, this life and this soul for the greatest possible good. And achieving the optimum balance and health of all of my bodies, opening my third eye, lifting the veil, igniting my light body, becoming the fullness of who I am, and *creating more of God's thought in all that I do* [repeat this last part three times].

Now I reach across to [name your family, friends, animals as you choose] and I pull into the light from all of *their* bodies every bit of negativity. And I pull into the light from all of their bodies anything that in any way will slow, hamper or prevent them achieving their life's goals, achieving the greater good, achieving the full potential of all of their bodies, and their learning and growing continuously. And I pull into the light anything that in any way will bring about harm, illness, pain or degeneration to any of their bodies.

Everything that's been pulled into the light I process into positive energy. [Vocal sequence here, toning from the heart.] And I send everything that's been pulled into the light down to my mother GAIA for her to continue processing into positive energy. [Imagine all of this emptying from you to mother GAIA.] I am a child of the earth, the earth nurtures and cares for me.

I reach up to my masters, teachers, guides, guardian angels […] my whole support team. I send up anything that will slow, hamper or prevent me becoming the fullness of who I am and having the free flow of abundance in all things. And I send them all of you love and light.

[Connecting]

I am surrounded by light, filled with light, I am light. I am surrounded by love, filled with love, I am love. I am surrounded by joy, filled with joy, I am joy. And I stream this light, love and joy down to my mother GAIA. [Visualize this] And I reach down to the core of the earth and pull up the silver and gold that is my mother [visual of DNA] and send it up to my support team [masters, teachers, guides, …] and then it is shared with my [husband, mother, father, sister, friends, animals, …] [Repeat this visualization of streaming down and pulling up three times as you say:] May this process continue day and night with every breath I take for as long as I live. I am a child of the earth, the earth nurtures and cares for me. I am a child of the earth, the earth nurtures and cares for me. I am a child of the earth, the earth nurtures and cares for me, and I nurture and care for her.

I am a child of the light. I am filled with light, surrounded by light, explode with light. [First toning] I am connected to all that is. [Spoken] And I am filled with love, joy, happiness, peace, health, strength, courage, wisdom and knowledge and I have bountifulness and abundance all of my life for as long as I may live.

I breathe up the light of the earth and connect to the light of the heavens. [Visualize the connection, breathing up the light of the earth, connecting to the light of the heavens and then each of your chakras exploding with love and light starting with your heart chakra, down an octave, and up an octave. Then visualize an opening lotus flower, and send the pedals one-by-one to those you love, those you protect. These are precious. Choose well.]

[Second toning] I am connected to all that is. [Spoken] And I am filled with love, joy, happiness, peace, health, strength, courage, wisdom and knowledge and I have bountifulness and abundance all of my life for as long as I may live. [Now blow this wonderful energy down into the core of Mother Earth.]

[Third toning] I am connected to all that is. [Spoken] And I am filled with love, joy, happiness, peace, health, strength, courage, wisdom and knowledge and I have bountifulness and abundance all of my life for as long as I may live. The light gives me the energy, ability, strength, courage, wisdom and knowledge to be all I can be, do all I can do, be the best person I can be in terms of the greater good. To always, always, always work toward the greater good. To live a long and healthy and happy life with [partner's name, family] and to fill that life, and the lives of our children and their families, the lives of our friends and animals, and all those who have touched or will touch Mountain Quest [choose your own associations] with love, joy, happiness, peace, health, strength, courage, wisdom and knowledge and may they have bountifulness and abundance all of their lives for as long as they may live.

[Offering Thanks]

I reach up to my masters, teachers, guides, higher Self, monad, Soul, angels [change/add according to your belief set]. Thank you, thank you, thank you, for all that you have done, all that you do, and all that you will do. [Touching eyes] Open my eyes that I may see; [touching ears] open my ears that I may hear; and [touching heart] open my heart that I may know and feel and love and be of greater service to the greater good.

[Reclaiming Power]

[Reaching hands upward] I open to the fullness of who I am [say 3 times]. I reclaim my power [say 3 times]. I am a creator [say 3 times], and I create love, joy, happiness, learning, growth, and light, and God's thought in all that I do, God's thought in all that I do, God's thought in all that I do. And I create health and healing in all of my bodies [and here name all those you desire to send light for health and healing, including Mother GAIA].

[Hands in front, palms up] The resources flow to me: Light, Love, Joy, Health, Opportunities, Knowledge, and Abundance in all things [repeat last phrase 3 times]. Wisdom, and Your help in all things [repeat last phrase 3 times].

[Refilling and Surrounding]

Now I fill Mountain Quest [change name to the place you live] with love and light and connect her to All That Is [visualize]. May all those come whom she can serve; may all those come who can serve her. May groups who resonate with her fill the Inn.

[Again, substitute as appropriate.] I fill the Inn with light, surround her with light, and send the light across the land. [Repeat same for other places, Mountain Quest Example: retreat center, old house, stable, barn.]

[Visualizing place] I send light to the earth, the air, the water, the fire. I send light to the spirits of the earth and ask for their help in watching over the people and animals on this land. I send light to every crystal, charge them, and ask for their help in watching over this land. I send light to all those advanced souls who have touched or will touch Mountain Quest. [Add any personal preferences … sending light to specific people, animals, etc.]

[Repeat these same two paragraphs for different places that you choose to fill and surround with light. For example, Alex does this, or a simpler version of this, for every place she works and teaches around the world. There are no limits. This can be a specific place, a city, or a country, sending light to specific people of your choice who live in these areas.]

[Closing]

[Raising hands.] I send light to all those who send light to the earth, and the 5th and 6th dimensional people who are leading our shift in consciousness. I connect to them with every thought, word, and act, every heartbeat, every breath. [Blowing breath in a circle and visualizing] I surround the earth with light, fill her with light, and send light to the orbs and energies around the earth. May only those advanced souls who seek the greater good come through this light [repeat this sentence 3 times]. [Same sequence two more times starting with "I surround the earth with light …..]

[Bringing hands to heart] My ego and personality merge with my self and my soul, and we merge with our Self and our Soul, and we use the collective wisdom of all that is (past, present and future) and all of our lives and all of our bodies to create more of God's thought in all that we do. Amen. Amen. Amen. And so it is; and so I let it be.

[Can close by (raising arms) sending light to the Universe, (crossing arms on chest) sending light to God, and (holding hands in front of you palms up) sending light to the orbs and energies that surround you.]

Appendix B: The First Visit with Mother Teresa

The following article was written by Alex Bennet (then Alex Dean) and originally appeared in the November 30, 1984, Seahawk, Vol. XXXV, No. 48, U.S. Fleet Activities, Yokosuka, Japan. Over the next few weeks this article was reprinted in U.S. Navy newspapers throughout the world. This visit to Camp Zama marked the first time Mother Teresa came onto a military base to speak. Alex, then Editor of the Seahawk, was invited to interview her and photograph the event. See Bennet, A. (2018), Possibilities that are YOU! Volume 4: Conscious Compassion, Frost, WV: MQIPress for a more detailed account of that experience.

Where will the peace begin? . . .

"It was one of those things that don't happen in a lifetime but happened to me," shared Col. Robert G. Garrett, Senior Chaplain at Camp Zama Chapel. "I can't say it's a once-in-a-lifetime experience because most people don't have it happen in their lifetime. It was one of those things that happen and I'm just happy to be a part of it."

Mother Teresa of Calcutta, 1979 Nobel Peace Prize recipient, appeared at the high school gymnasium in Camp Zama on Tuesday evening, November 20 [1984]. Her day was a long one. She spoke earlier at the International school in Tokyo, then visited a hospital in Hamamatsu. A U.S. Army C-12 flew her to Atsugi (with the Navy standing by as backup), then she was heloed to Camp Zama.

Greeting Mother at Camp Zama Chapel was a welcoming committee comprised of individuals who have worked with her mission in Tokyo. Mother was accompanied by Father Andre Bogaert and Sister Chiba. Following a warm exchange, all joined in a dinner of chicken, baked beans, bread and Indian tea with sugar and cream.

Mother Teresa was born August 27, 1910, in what is now Yugoslavia. In an interview she stated, "At the age of twelve I first knew I had a vocation to help the poor." During her eighteenth year she left to join the Sisters of Loretto, a community of Irish nuns with a mission in the Archdiocese of Calcutta. She took her first vows as a nun in 1928 and her final vows nine years later.

During her work of teaching and serving as principal at St. Mary's High School in Calcutta, her heart was greatly touched by the suffering children, lepers, and destitute ill outside the cloister walls. In 1946 she received a "call within a call." "The message was clear. I was to leave the convent and help the poor, while living among them."

In 1948 Mother Teresa founded the Society of the Missionaries of Charity in Calcutta's slums. Since that time she has "worked unstintingly to bring aid and dignity to the destitute and dying" both in her adopted country, India, and in more than 25 countries worldwide.

Twelve hundred expectant faces awaited her appearance in the Camp Zama gymnasium. They were not disappointed. The 73-year-old, slight form entered the side door, paused to exchange smiles with a young child, and with back bowed and hands clasped in front of her, edged gracefully up the stairs onto an appropriately placed platform.

Mother Teresa spoke. Softly. Vibrantly.

"We hear in the scripture that God loved the world so much that He gave his son Jesus to come into this world and bring us the good news that He loves the world. That He loves you and He loves me and He loves that leper …

"A few weeks ago, two young people came to our house. They gave me lots of money and I asked them where do you get so much money? They said two days ago we got married and before we married we decided to have no wedding feast. To have no wedding clothes. To give the money to you to feed the people, your people. I was surprised and asked them about it. They answered, 'We wanted to share the joy of love by giving' …

"Hunger is not for bread alone. Hunger is for love. Hunger is for the word of God …

"I will never forget one day walking down a street in London. I saw a man sitting looking very lonely, so I went right up to him. I reached for his hands. They were so cold. He looked up at me and said, 'After such a long time I'm feeling the warmth of a human hand.' And he had a smile on his face because there was someone who loved him …

"Small things are special to us … Today people are so terribly busy that they have no time to even smile at each other … God speaks in the silence of the heart …

"The world has never needed peace so much as today. Where will the peace begin? …

"A few days before I came here a poor man came to our house, a poor man from the slums, and he said his only child was dying and the doctor had prescribed this special medicine that could be gotten only from England. I said I would do what I could. He gave me the prescription. Just at that moment a man came in with a basket of medicine. We have people that we send to families and they gather the leftover medicines from the people of Calcutta. This man came with the basket of half-used medicine and what was on the top of all the medicines—that medicine, the one that the doctor has prescribed.

"Had he come before, had he come after, I would not have seen him. But he came just at that moment.

"Out of millions and millions and millions of children in the world, God was concerned for that little boy in Calcutta. God's concern for us is so great …

"I will pray for you, for your families, for the work you have to do. I will pray for you that you grow in holiness. For holiness is not the luxury of the few. It is the simple duty for every one of us …

"I'll pray for you and you pray for me. God bless you."

There were twelve hundred people pushing (gently) to reach her hand. Others, who had already done so, struggled to retreat through the crowd, faces glowing with thoughtfulness.

It was nearly an impossible task to photograph her: heads and hands bobbed constantly in and out of the field. Then I was right there in front of her, a young girl beside me reached out to Mother and pressed Mother's hand against her cheek. Then those sparkling dark eyes in their small earth-worn frame turned to me.

The twelve hundred disappeared. My hand reached towards her; the camera dropped to the length of its neck strap. Her grasp was firm and carried with it a warmth that tingled my knuckles and spread rapidly up my forearm.

Our locked eyes reached beyond the soft pushing and struggling of the moment, and continued into our very souls. I do not know what she found; I discovered a love so deep, a giving so great ...

There was no hurry. Seconds became hours. There was a great contentment within me; a wonderful feeling of being at peace with myself. Mother's hand was never withdrawn from mine, yet she was reaching for another … She had shared her life experiences and understanding specifically with me—yet we had not exchanged a word.

About the Mountain Quest Institute

MQI is a research, retreat and learning center dedicated to helping individuals achieve personal and professional growth and organizations create and sustain high performance in a rapidly changing, uncertain, and increasingly complex world. Drs. David and Alex Bennet are co-founders of MQI. They may be contacted at alex@mountainquestinstitute.com

Current research is focused on Human and Organizational Systems, Change, Complexity, Sustainability, Knowledge, Learning, Consciousness, and the nexus of Science and Spirituality. MQI has three questions: The Quest for Knowledge, The Quest for Consciousness, and The Quest for Meaning. **MQI is scientific, humanistic and spiritual and finds no contradiction in this combination**. See www.mountainquestinstitute.com

MQI is the birthplace of Organizational Survival in the New World: The Intelligent Complex Adaptive System (Elsevier, 2004), a new theory of the firm that turns the living system metaphor into a reality for organizations. Based on research in complexity and neuroscience—and incorporating networking theory and knowledge management—this book is filled with new ideas married to practical advice, all embedded within a thorough description of the new organization in terms of structure, culture, strategy, leadership, knowledge workers and integrative competencies.

Mountain Quest Institute, situated four hours from Washington, D.C. in the Monongahela Forest of the Allegheny Mountains, is part of the Mountain Quest complex which includes a Retreat Center, Inn, and the old Farm House, Outbuildings and mountain trails and farmland. See www.moountainquestinn.com The Retreat Center is designed to provide full learning experiences, including hosting training, workshops, retreats and business meetings for professional and executive groups of 25 people or less. The Center includes a 26,000 volume research library, a conference room, community center, computer room, 12 themed bedrooms, a workout and hot tub area, and a four-story tower with a glass ceiling for enjoying the magnificent view of the valley during the day and the stars at night. Situated on a 430 acres farm, there is a labyrinth, creeks, four miles of mountain trails, and horses, Longhorn cattle, Llamas and a myriad of wild neighbors. Other neighbors include the Snowshoe Ski Resort, the National Radio Astronomy Observatory and the CASS Railroad.

About the Authors

Dr. Alex Bennet, a Professor at the Bangkok University Institute for Knowledge and Innovation Management, is internationally recognized as an expert in knowledge management and an agent for organizational change. Prior to founding the Mountain Quest Institute, she served as the Chief Knowledge Officer and Deputy Chief Information Officer for Enterprise Integration for the U.S. Department of the Navy, and was co-chair of the Federal Knowledge Management Working Group. Dr. Bennet is the recipient of the Distinguished and Superior Public Service Awards from the U.S. government for her work in the Federal Sector. She is a Delta Epsilon Sigma and Golden Key National Honor Society graduate with a Ph.D. in Human and Organizational Systems; degrees in Management for Organizational Effectiveness, Human Development, English and Marketing; and certificates in Total Quality Management, System Dynamics and Defense Acquisition Management. Alex believes in the multidimensionality of humanity as we move out of infancy into full consciousness.

Dr. David Bennet's experience spans many years of service in the Military, Civil Service and Private Industry, including fundamental research in underwater acoustics and nuclear physics, frequent design and facilitation of organizational interventions, and serving as technical director of two major DoD Acquisition programs. Prior to founding the Mountain Quest Institute, Dr. Bennet was CEO, then Chairman of the Board and Chief Knowledge Officer of a professional services firm located in Alexandria, Virginia. He is a Phi Beta Kappa, Sigma Pi Sigma, and Suma Cum Laude graduate of the University of Texas, and holds degrees in Mathematics, Physics, Nuclear Physics, Liberal Arts, Human and Organizational Development, and a Ph.D. in Human Development focused on Neuroscience and adult learning. He is currently researching the nexus of Science, the Humanities and Spirituality.

Also available ...

Possibilities that are YOU! by Alex Bennet

This series of short books, which are published under *Conscious Look Books*, are conversational in nature, taking full advantage of your lived experience to share what can sometimes be difficult concepts to grab onto. But, **YOU ARE READY!** We live in a world that is tearing itself apart, where people are out of control, rebelling from years of real and perceived abuse and suppression of thought. Yet, this chaos offers us as a humanity the opportunity to make a giant leap forward. *By opening ourselves to ourselves, we are able to fully explore who we are and who we can become.* With that exploration comes a glimmer of hope as we begin to reclaim the power of each and every mind developed by the lived human experience!

These books share 22 large concepts from *The Profundity and Bifurcation of Change*. Each book includes seven ideas offered for the student of life experience to help you become the co-creator you are. Available in soft cover from Amazon.

Titles:

All Things in Balance
The Art of Thought Adjusting
Associative Patterning and Attracting
Beyond Action
The Bifurcation
Connections as Patterns
Conscious Compassion
The Creative Leap
The Emerging Self
The Emoting Guidance System
Engaging Forces
The ERC's of Intuition
Grounding
The Humanness of Humility
Intention and Attention
Knowing
Living Virtues for Today
ME as Co-Creator
Seeking Wisdom
Staying on the Path
Transcendent Beauty
Truth in Context

*A   A 23rd little book titled **The Intelligent Social Change Journey** provides the theoretical foundation for the **Possibilities that are YOU! series.** Available in soft cover from Amazon*

Other Books by these authors from MQI Press

MQIPress is a wholly-owned subsidiary of Mountain Quest Institute, LLC, located at 303 Mountain Quest Lane, Marlinton, West Virginia 24954, USA. (304) 799-7267

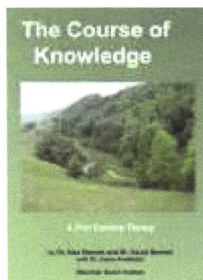

The Course of Knowledge: A 21st Century Theory
by Alex Bennet and David Bennet with Joyce Avedisian (2015)

Knowledge is at the core of what it is to be human, the substance which informs our thoughts and determines the course of our actions. Our growing focus on, and understanding of, knowledge and its consequent actions is changing our relationship with the world. Because **knowledge determines the quality of every single decision we make**, it is critical to learn about and understand what knowledge is. **From a 21st century viewpoint,** we explore a theory of knowledge that is both pragmatic and biological. Pragmatic in that it is based on taking effective action, and biological because it is created by humans via patterns of neuronal connections in the mind/brain.

In this book we explore *the course of knowledge.* Just as a winding stream in the bowls of the mountains curves and dips through ravines and high valleys, so, too, with knowledge. In a continuous journey towards intelligent activity, context-sensitive and situation-dependent knowledge, imperfect and incomplete, experientially engages a changing landscape in a continuous cycle of learning and expanding. *We are in a continuous cycle of knowledge creation such that every moment offers the opportunity for the emergence of new and exciting ideas, all waiting to be put in service to an interconnected world.* Learn more about this **exciting human capacity**! AVAILABLE FROM AMAZON in softback cover and as an eBook.

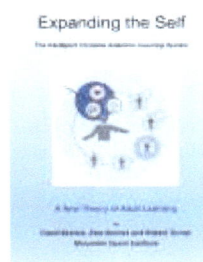

Expanding the Self: The Intelligent Complex Adaptive Learning System
by David Bennet, Alex Bennet and Robert Turner (2015)

We live in unprecedented times; indeed, turbulent times that can arguably be defined as ushering humanity into a new Golden Age, offering the opportunity to embrace new ways of learning and living in a globally and collaboratively entangled connectedness. In this shifting and dynamic environment, life demands accelerated cycles of learning experiences. Fortunately, we as a humanity have begun to look within ourselves to better understand the way our mind/brain operates, the amazing qualities of the body that power our thoughts and feelings, and the reciprocal loops as those thoughts and feelings change our physical structure. This emerging knowledge begs us to relook and rethink what we know about learning.

This book is a treasure for those interested in how recent findings in neuroscience impact learning. The result of this work is an expanding **experiential learning model called the Intelligent Complex Adaptive Learning System**, adding the **fifth mode of social engagement** to Kolb's concrete experience, reflective observation, abstract conceptualization and active experimentation, with the five modes undergirded by **the power of Self**. A significant conclusion is that should they desire, adults have much more control over their learning than they may realize. AVAILABLE FROM AMAZON in softback cover and as an eBook.

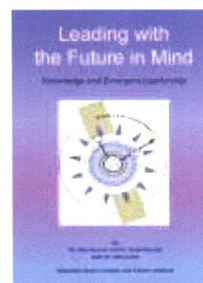

Leading with the Future in Mind: Knowledge and Emergent Leadership
by Alex Bennet and David Bennet with John Lewis (2015)

We exist in a new reality, a global world where the individuated power of the mind/brain offers possibilities beyond our imagination. It is within this framework that thought leading emerges, and when married to our collaborative nature, makes the impossible an everyday occurrence. *Leading with the Future in Mind*, **building on profound insights unleashed by recent findings in neuroscience**, provides a new view that converges leadership, knowledge and learning for individual and organizational advancement.
This book provides a **research-based** *tour de force* **for the future of leadership**. Moving from the leadership of the past, for the few at the top, using authority as the explanation, we now find leadership emerging from all levels of the organization, with knowledge as the explanation. The future will be owned by the organizations that can master the relationships between knowledge and leadership. Wrapped in the mantle of collaboration and engaging our full resources—physical, mental, emotional and spiritual—we open the door to possibilities. We are dreaming the future together. AVAILABLE FROM AMAZON in softback cover and as an eBook.

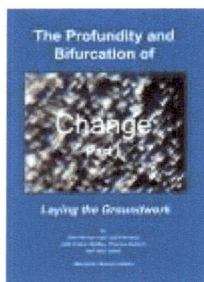

The Profundity and Bifurcation of Change Part I: Laying the Groundwork
by Alex Bennet and David Bennet with Arthur Shelley, Theresa Bullard and John Lewis

This book lays the groundwork for the **Intelligent Social Change Journey** (ISCJ), a developmental journey of the body, mind and heart, moving from the heaviness of cause-and-effect linear extrapolations, to the fluidity of co-evolving with our environment, to the lightness of breathing our thought and feelings into reality. Grounded in development of our mental faculties, these are phase changes, each building on and expanding previous learning in our movement toward intelligent activity. As we lay the groundwork, we move through the concepts of change, knowledge, forces, self and consciousness. Then, recognizing that we are holistic beings, we provide a baseline model for individual change from within.

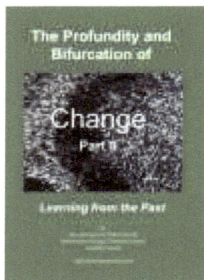

The Profundity and Bifurcation of Change Part II: Learning from the Past
by Alex Bennet and David Bennet with Arthur Shelley, Theresa Bullard and John Lewis

Phase 1 of the Intelligent Social Change Journey (ISCJ) is focused on the linear cause-and-effect relationships of logical thinking. Knowledge, situation dependent and context sensitive, is a product of the past. **Phase 1 assumes that for every effect there is an originating cause.** This is where we as a humanity, and as individuals, begin to develop our mental faculties. In this book we explore cause and effect, scan a kaleidoscope of change models, and review the modalities of change. Since change is easier and more fluid when we are grounded, we explore three interpretations of grounding. In preparation for expanding our consciousness, a readiness assessment and sample change agent's strategy are included. (Release 01/15/17)

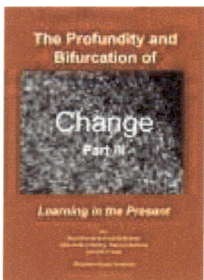

The Profundity and Bifurcation of Change Part III: Learning in the Present
by Alex Bennet and David Bennet with Arthur Shelley, Theresa Bullard and John Lewis

As the world becomes increasingly complex, Phase 2 of the Intelligent Social Change Journey (ISCJ) is focused on **co-evolving with the environment**. This requires a deepening connection to others, moving into empathy. While the NOW is the focus, there is an increasing ability to put together patterns from the past and think conceptually, as well as extrapolate future behaviors. Thus, we look closely at the relationship of time and space, and pattern thinking. We look at the human body as a complex energetic system, exploring the role of emotions as a guidance system, and what happens when we have stuck energy. This book also introduces Knowledge Capacities, different ways of thinking that build capacity for sustainability.

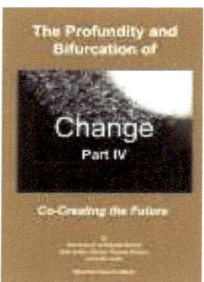

The Profundity and Bifurcation of Change Part IV: Co-Creating the Future
by Alex Bennet and David Bennet with Arthur Shelley, Theresa Bullard and John Lewis

As we move into Phase 3 of the Intelligent Social Change Journey (ISCJ), **we fully embrace our role as co-creator**. We recognize the power of thought and the role of attention and intention in our ever-expanding search for a higher level of truth. Whether we choose to engage it or not, we explore mental discipline as a tool toward expanded consciousness. In preparing ourselves for the creative leap, there are ever-deepening connections with others. We now understand that the mental faculties are in service to the intuitional, preparing us to, and expanding our ability to, act in and on the world, living with conscious compassion and tapping into the intuitional at will.

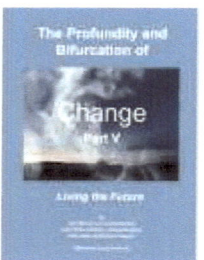

The Profundity and Bifurcation of Change Part V: Living the Future
by Alex Bennet and David Bennet with Arthur Shelley, Theresa Bullard, John Lewis and Donna Panucci

We embrace the ancient art and science of Alchemy to **explore the larger shift underway for humanity** and how we can consciously and intentionally speed up evolution to enhance outcomes. In this conversation, we look at balancing and sensing, the harmony of beauty, and virtues for living the future. Conscious compassion, a virtue, is introduced as a state of being connected to morality and good character, inclusive of giving selfless service. We are now ready to refocus our attention on knowledge and consciousness, exploring their new roles in our advancement. And all of this expanding and growth as we move through the ISCJ is giving a wide freedom of choice as we approach the bifurcation. What will we manifest?

REMEMBRANCE: Pathways to Expanded Learning with Music and Metamusic®
by Barbara Bullard and Alex Bennet (2013)

Take **a journey of discovery into the last great frontier—the human mind/brain**, an instrument of amazing flexibility and plasticity. This eBook is written for brain users who are intent on mining more of the golden possibilities that lie inherent in each of our unique brains. Begin by discovering the role positive attitudes play in learning, and the power of self-affirmations and visualizations. Then explore the use of brain wave entrainment mixed with designer music called Metamusic® to achieve enhanced learning states. Join students of all ages who are **creating magical learning outcomes using music and Metamusic.®** AVAILABLE FROM AMAZON in softback cover and as an eBook.

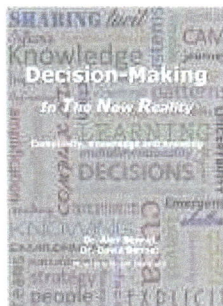

Decision-Making in The New Reality: Complexity, Knowledge and Knowing
by Alex Bennet and David Bennet (2013)

We live in a world that offers many possible futures. The ever-expanding complexity of information and knowledge provide many choices for decision-makers, and we are all making decisions every single day! As the problems and messes of the world become more complex, our decision consequences are more and more difficult to anticipate, and our **decision-making processes must change to keep up with this world complexification**. This book takes a consilience approach to explore decision-making in The New Reality, fully engaging systems and complexity theory, knowledge research, and recent neuroscience findings. It also presents methodologies for decision-makers to tap into their unconscious, accessing tacit knowledge resources and increasingly relying on the sense of knowing that is available to each of us.

Almost every day new energies are erupting around the world: new thoughts, new feelings, new knowing, all contributing to new situations that require new decisions and actions from each and every one of us. A global consciousness is emerging. As complex adaptive systems linked to a flowing fount of knowing, we can each bring these resources to bear to achieve our ever-expanding vision of the future. Are we up to the challenge? AVAILABLE FROM AMAZON in softback cover and as an eBook.

Other Books by these authors

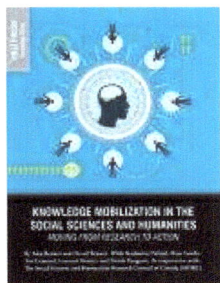

Knowledge Mobilization in the Social Sciences and Humanities: Moving from Research to Action *by Alex Bennet and David Bennet* (2007)

This book takes the reader from the University lab to the playgrounds of communities. It shows how to integrate, move and use knowledge, an action journey within an identified action space that is called knowledge mobilization. Whether knowledge is mobilized through an individual, organization, community or nation, it becomes **a powerful asset** creating a synergy and focus that brings forth the best of action and values. Individuals and teams who can envision, feel, create and apply this power are the true leaders of tomorrow. When we can **mobilize knowledge for the greater good** humanity will have left the information age and entered the age of knowledge, ultimately leading to compassion and—hopefully—wisdom. AVAILABLE FROM AMAZON as an eBook and softback cover (used).

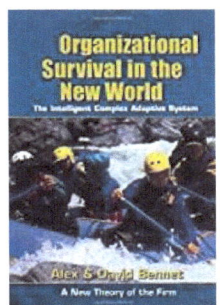

Organizational Survival in the New World: The Intelligent Complex Adaptive System
by Alex Bennet and David Bennet (Elsevier, 2004), available in hard and soft formats from Amazon.

In this book the Bennets propose a new model for organizations that enables them to react more quickly and fluidly to today's fast-changing, dynamic business environment: The Intelligent Complex Adaptive System (ICAS). ICAS is a new organic model of the firm based on recent research in complexity and neuroscience, and incorporating networking theory and knowledge management, turning the living system metaphor into a reality for organizations. This book synthesizes new thinking about organizational structure and provides a **new systems model for the successful organization of the future** designed to help leaders and managers of knowledge organizations succeed in a non-linear, complex, fast-changing and turbulent environment. AVAILABLE FROM AMAZON in hard cover, softback cover and as an eBook.

The Myst Series

(available in softback cover and as eBooks)

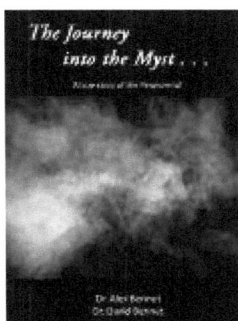

The Journey into the Myst ... A true story of the Paranormal (Volume I)
by Alex Bennet and David Bennet

"What we are about to tell you would have been quite unbelievable to me before this journey began. It is not a story of the reality either of us has known for well over our 60 and 70 years of age, but rather, the reality of dreams and fairytales." This is the true story of a sequence of events that happened at Mountain Quest, situated in a high valley of the Allegheny Mountains of West Virginia. **The story begins with a miracle**, expanding into the capture and cataloging of thousands of pictures of electromagnetic spheres widely known as "orbs." **This joyous experience became an exploration into the unknown** with the emergence of what the author's fondly call the *Myst*, the forming and shaping of non-random patterns such as human faces, angels and animals. As this phenomenon unfolds, you will discover how the Drs. Alex and David Bennet began to observe and interact with the *Myst*. This book shares the beginning of an extraordinary *Journey into the Myst*. AVAILABLE in softcover and as an eBook.

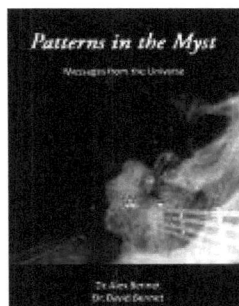

Patterns in the Myst: Messages from the Universe (Volume II)
by Alex Bennet and David Bennet

The Journey into the Myst was just the beginning for Drs. Alex and David Bennet. Volume II of the Myst Series brings Science into the Spiritual experience, bringing to bear what the Bennets have learned through their research and educational experiences in physics, neuroscience, human systems, knowledge management and human development. Embracing the paralogical, **patterns in the *Myst* are observed, felt, interpreted, analyzed and compared** in terms of their physical make-up, non-randomness, intelligent sources and potential implications. Along the way, the Bennets were provided amazing pictures reflecting the forming of the Myst. AVAILABLE in softcover and as an eBook.

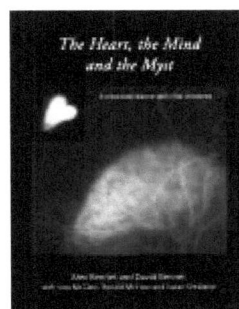

The Heart, the Mind and the Myst: A Neuronal Dance with the Universe (Volume III)
by Alex Bennet and David Bennet with Sara McClain, Ronald McClain and Susan Dreiband

The Bennets shift to introspection in this third volume of the series to explore the continuing impact of the *Myst* experience on the human psyche. Joined by several co-authors, the book unfolds the experiences of a handful of people whose lives have become entangled with the *Myst* phenomenon. So many questions have come to mind over the experiential years in the *Myst*. How does this amazing experience change our beliefs and values? Do we feel and think differently? Do we act differently? What have we learned? And finally, as humanity has entered the shifting times of the 2020's, **how has this experience prepared us for the changes underway today?** AVAILABLE in softcover.

www.ingramcontent.com/pod-product-compliance
Lightning Source LLC
Chambersburg PA
CBHW060812090426
42737CB00002B/40